Enjoy! Merry Christmas
Jo-Ann & Bruce
12/08

The Hemi in the Barn

The Hemi in the Barn

More Great Stories of Automotive Archaeology

TOM COTTER

FOREWORD BY JAY LENO

MOTORBOOKS

DEDICATION

To Dick Bauer, who believed this furniture salesman could become a PR guy and a writer.

First published in 2007 by Motorbooks, an imprint of MBI Publishing Company, Galtier Plaza, Suite 200, 380 Jackson Street, St. Paul, MN 55101 USA

Motorbooks titles are also available at discounts in bulk quantity for industrial or sales-promotional use. For details write to Special Sales Manager at MBI Publishing Company, Galtier Plaza, Suite 200, 380 Jackson Street, St. Paul, MN 55101 USA.

To find out more about our books, join us online at www.motorbooks.com.

Library of Congress Cataloging-in-Publication Data

Cotter, Tom, 1954-
The Hemi in the barn : more great stories of automotive archaeology / by Tom Cotter; foreword by Jay Leno.
p. cm.
ISBN-13: 978-0-7603-2721-0 (hardbound w/ jacket)
1. Antique and classic cars--Anecdotes. I. Title.
TL7.A1C685 2007
629.222--dc22

Editors: Lee Klancher and Leah Noel
Designer: Tom Heffron

Printed in China

On the front cover, main: An unreliable source led to the discovery of this Plymouth Superbird hidden in a hedge in an Alabama backyard. Barry Lee now is the owner of this muscle car—one of only 1,920 built. *Bill Warner*

On the front cover, inset: A dilapidated 1939 Ford convertible that was once a sixteen-year-old's sweet ride. *Russ Roberts*

On the back cover: A rare Jaguar SSI, once owned by Prince and Princess Pignatelli of Italy, which was found in a Connecticut garage. *Mike Covello*

Contents

FOREWORD

"Everything has its beauty, but
not everyone sees it." — Confucius

BY JAY LENO

Every enthusiast dreams about finding a long-lost car in a garage or a barn. It doesn't happen very often. I think if you just go out looking for cars, and not for any particular car, you're more likely to find something you want.

I think all the Duesenbergs have been discovered; probably all the Cobras have been accounted for; and all the C-Jags and the D-Jags are pretty much known. But there are still a lot of other exciting cars out there.

The fun part of my job is that because I'm on *The Tonight Show*, people think they know me. So they send me notes or letters, and 99 percent of the time they say, "I have a very rare 1976 Ford Granada—one of the only ones with the full wire wheel hubcaps." Every now and then, though, there's something that's a little bit more interesting. It usually comes from an older person, and that's my point.

If you're looking for old cars, I recommend that you talk to old guys. They were all young guys once. A lot of them don't have children; they don't have any family left. They just want to see the love of their life, the car they were *always* going to restore (but never got around to it), go to a good home.

And although price is always a consideration, for a lot of guys, it's not the *main* consideration. So you go around to old folks' homes, and you talk to old people. It's like "Hey, didja ever have an old car?" And they might say: "Oh yeah, the people next door to us had an old car. Now what the hell was that?"

So you go there, and maybe it's something cool, like a '49 Nash Airflyte. Maybe it's a long-forgotten Hudson Hornet.

If you enjoy doing the legwork, the detective work, it's no different than going antiquing with your wife on a Saturday afternoon. It's just that you're doin' it with cars.

One thing I've found is that a lot of old guys just want somebody to talk to. They might keep you on a string forever. But that's OK. They *are* fun to talk to, and you might just discover something.

If you like cars, but only D-Jags, Cobras, and muscle cars, then you don't really *like* cars. But if you like anything that has an interesting story, then you're really an enthusiast.

Consider my '51 Hudson Hornet. I got a letter from an elderly woman in her 90s; she'd gotten married in this car. In fact, it was the only car she and her husband ever had. After he died in 1996, it was parked in her garage. I went to look at it. Physically, it was fine. Mechanically, it was worn out. It had gone 260,000 miles. But it was all there. Every receipt was in the glove compartment. So I bought the story more than I bought the car.

The real trick is not to be disappointed if what you find isn't some rare collector piece. Let's say you find a '56 Chevy or a '55 Ford two-door, three-on-the-tree 292-cubic-inch V-8. These cars are fun to drive. They give you a driving experience that can't be duplicated today. You can get cars like this from anywhere from $2,500 to $5,500, and with a little bit of elbow grease, you have a collector car that's a lot of fun.

And, there may be a great story behind it.

Any car can be a collector car, if *you* collect it. People always say buy the best car you can and do all this kind of nonsense. That's nice, if you're rich. But a friend of mine has a Bugatti. It's completely rotted out. You couldn't possibly restore it. But he bought it; now he's in the Bugatti Club. This car is literally a burned-out hulk. It would take a gazillion dollars to restore it. But he can say he's got a Bugatti!

If you're an investor, you might not be interested in a lot of barn finds. But you may be missing out. Take a '66 Ford LTD—it's a fun, unusual car that somebody loved at one time, and maybe they locked it away. You can rescue it.

If you're looking for an old car someone's tucked away, the best advice I can give is to find the oldest garage or gas station in your town. Talk to the guy who runs it. Ask him if there are any customers who haven't been in for a long time. Do they have an interesting car? Maybe there's a '69 Bonneville or something even older, just waiting to be discovered.

If you like old things, go to old people. Seek them out. Go to the places where old hot rodders used to hang out; join the car clubs. Be polite, but be persistent.

There are people who'd like you to have their old car. You just have to find them.

That's why I liked Tom Cotter's first book on barn finds, *The Cobra in the Barn*. This book really struck a chord with me. There are diet books and self-help books out there, but they have no real effect on me. Tom's book, on the other hand, is genuinely fun and interesting to read. And that's rare.

Every car enthusiast dreams about finding an old car in a barn. I've been lucky to find a few cars that way, and two of those stories are in this book. Sometimes "barn finds" are valuable; sometimes they're not. But they're usually great stories.

Tom Cotter shared those stories in his first book, and he's done it again with this one.

I hope you enjoy it as much as I did.

Jay Leno is the host of The Tonight Show.

ACKNOWLEDGMENTS

Thanks to all who contributed their stories for this book, whether they were used or not. Special thanks to my magazine friends—Steve Spence, Don Sherman, Paul Duchene, Tim Suddard, Peter Brock, and Mike Covello—who allowed me to tap into their terrific stories that had previously been published. And my heartfelt thanks to Bill Warner, Ken Gross, Jay Leno, Lee Klancher, Leah Noel, and my family, Pat and Brian Cotter. Thank you all for your assistance, patience, and support.

INTRODUCTION

"Most people discover old cars while looking at scenery;
I discover scenery while looking for old cars."

The Cobra in the Barn was a fluke. At least I thought so. I mean, who would want to read a bunch of stories about a group of social misfits who get their kicks from searching for rusting relics? But not long after that book was published in 2005, I started to get e-mail messages and packages from others who were as addicted to "the search" as I was.

I heard hearty thank yous from many folks, saying that since a book had been published on barn finding, perhaps their passion now seemed more legitimate to their families and friends. Glad to help you.

Barn finding is an addiction. I can't go on a business trip, vacation, to a wedding, or funeral—heck, I can't even go out for a gallon of milk—without looking down driveways and behind garages. I just love the hunt, and gladly, I've discovered that I'm not alone.

I have decided that searching for old cars helps satisfy the yearnings we all had as twelve-year-olds, when a perfect Saturday was spent searching for pirate's treasure. As adults, our lives become complicated with work and family responsibilities, so we reach back—either consciously or unconsciously—to more simple endeavors . . . like those enjoyed by our twelve-year-old selves.

Thankfully, you, the reader, seem to enjoy the stories regardless of the brand of car mentioned in the tale. I've come to appreciate that the cars are simply catalysts for great human interest stories.

The first book sold well enough that my publisher, Motorbooks, asked me to do a sequel, which you are holding in your hands. Printed in the back of *The Cobra in the Barn*, almost hidden, was a small note that basically said if you have an interesting barn-find story, please contact me. The floodgates opened and great stories came across the transom. So this time, we're not hiding the notice; if you know of a great barn-find story and would like it considered, send it to: tcotter@cobrainthebarn.com.

Please remember, a great car with a mediocre story is not as desirable as a mediocre car with a great story. In the meantime, you enjoy the book, and I'll enjoy reading your stories.

— Tom Cotter, March 2007

CHAPTER ONE

Exotic Destinations

The Baltic Bulletproof Aktion P

BY STEVE SPENCE
MANAGING EDITOR, *CAR AND DRIVER*

On May 27, 1942, the second-most despised man in all of Nazi-occupied Czechoslovakia, General Reinhard Heydrich, was being chauffeured in an open Mercedes to his quarters in Prague's Hradcany Castle. At a bend in the road, two men waited for him. One was Josef Gabcik, who concealed a submachine gun under a raincoat, and the other was Jan Kubis, whose briefcase held two grenades.

The Mercedes 320 Cabriolet B was an hour late when it finally appeared. Gabcik stepped off the curb and into the path of the oncoming car. When the driver instinctively hit the brakes,

The bare aluminum shell that once stopped bullets. The Aktion P was once equipped with armor-plated sides, floor, and roof panels. The windshield and side windows could also stop a flying bullet. There is only one other Atkion P known in existence and its estimated worth is $20 million. *D. Randy Riggs*

Heydrich leaped to his feet and shouted at him to go on. Heydrich, known as "the Hangman of Europe," had vast experience in terror and killing, and he knew what was about to happen.

The trained assassin was not having a good day. With Heydrich in his sights, Gabcik's gun jammed. The Nazi general, frantic and yelling, freed his sidearm from its holster and fired wildly at Gabcik, who dropped the gun and ran. Kubis stepped up and lofted a grenade at the car. Heydrich was hit and collapsed on the street. After eight reputedly painful days, he died.

In retaliation, the Nazis slaughtered the male inhabitants of Lidice, a village thought to have sheltered the assassins. Hitler then ordered Daimler-Benz to produce some closed, bulletproof cars—twenty supercharged 540K models, called Aktion P cars (the P for panzer, or armored vehicle). The cars were built to safeguard Hitler's inner circle—Nazis like Himmler, Goebbels, Speer, and Kaltenbrunner.

Daimler complied by using two new chassis and rebodying eighteen 540Ks, some confiscated from existing owners. New aluminum bodies were built for all twenty cars, featuring 35-millimeter-thick bulletproof windshields, 30-millimeter side glass, and 2.3-millimeter steel armor plating lining the sides, floor, and roof. At war's end, most of their infamous occupants had either committed suicide or wound up at the end of a rope in Nuremberg. The cars wound up being treated as Nazi trash. Misused and discarded, they vanished into the fog of history.

Now, five decades later, a time when rare old cars are worth fortunes, only one Aktion P is known to have survived, and it resides, fittingly, in a museum in Czechoslovakia.

You can see it in the Holocaust film *Schindler's List*. It is not a spectacular car, like the other 540K convertibles, but its rarity makes it worth millions. A curator at the Mercedes-Benz museum, perhaps a bit too generously, guessed it might be worth $20 million.

It was no surprise that Peter the Swede would be the one to find the car. Peter looked tough—the leathery face, the wiry physique, a biker ponytail—and was fearless in strange foreign places. Then again, after you've spent nine months at the mercy of some sadistic anti-Western Arabs in a Libyan jail—most of the time naked, it was said—the world is no longer a scary place.

Peter the Swede had been around, even lived for a while in the United States. His talent was that people seemed to trust him immediately. Well, maybe insurance companies didn't. In the mid-1980s, he was picked up by the Libyans in the sea off Tripoli after scuttling a boat for an owner who was after the insurance money. But people did trust him.

In the summer of 1992, he walked into a town in Latvia, a former Soviet-bloc country west of Moscow, struck up conversations with strangers—even though he didn't speak the language—and ended up being invited to spend the night on somebody's sofa.

By poking around in that Baltic town, asking the right questions in his friendly and cheerful way, Peter the Swede found the car hiding in the countryside. He eventually led three Americans to a stonewalled barn that contained the jackpot car.

Actually, the car was in two houses and four barns.

Back in America that same summer of 1992, an aspiring hustler was dangling rare-automobile bait over the phone to Dick Fritz. It was a fool's errand. An exotic dealer in his fifties when this book was published, Fritz once worked in Ferrari's main American office and became a major player in the automotive "gray market" (altering foreign cars to meet U.S. regulations via his Amerispec Corporation in Connecticut).

The hustler we'll call "Barry of Memphis." He had an American partner in Moscow named Bud, who, he said, could lead Fritz to "hundreds" of valuable old cars, mostly Mercedes-Benzes pirated from Germany by the Red Army at the end of World War II.

With the collector-car market in a coma since its collapse in 1990, Fritz was ripe for a hunting expedition. And he knew that the notion of stumbling across a million-dollar car in a field, or in a barn, was not a myth.

Fritz relayed the hustler's story to one of his business contacts, an independently wealthy Yankee gentleman we'll call Brewster, who quickly offered to finance an expedition. A third partner was brought in—Rich Reuter, a third-generation car restorer from Danbury, Connecticut, who could tell at a glance if a rusting old hulk had a future—and a deal was struck.

The new partners flew Barry of Memphis up to Connecticut to see if he was real or fake. Barry brought more bait: snapshots from Moscow of three cars he and his partner had "already bought," a prewar Horch four-door convertible and two prewar Mercedes—a cabriolet and a roadster. Very nice cars, they all agreed.

Barry said he was going to Moscow soon. Fritz said he would put together a trip with his partners and meet Barry and his partner. Brewster would pay $10,000 for the trip to Russia and bring along $50,000 in cash. On June 24, 1992, the hunt began.

The cash they carried was a constant source of anxiety. Fritz said they tried to camouflage their nationality by dressing in not-so-nice clothes. Moscow had a predatory feel to it—news of murder and the Russian mafia were commonplace—and the group only went out at night to eat. The food was laughably bad. Their favorite restaurant, though expensive for Russians, was the Moscow McDonald's.

Barry and Bud had promised to meet the Americans at their hotel on the second day, but the pair never appeared.

Fritz, Reuter, and Brewster had made a few other contacts, and thus began a series of fruitless, comic excursions in search of old cars. Fritz videotaped these, though the plot seemed always the same: The camera records a dismal cityscape flying by, then a procession of interpreter, the driver, and the Americans filing through some junk-filled inner courtyard, coming ultimately upon a crumbling hulk. The original engine always seems to be missing, replaced by what appears to be a Soviet tractor engine. Inside, the floorboards might be covered by peeling kitchen linoleum, or there are gaping holes in the floorboards. Or flowered drapery is sewn into the door panels, or maybe the bumpers have been swapped, or the trunk lid is gone. The Russian owners are typically haggard and clad in grimy clothes, claiming relentlessly that everything in the car is "a-rig-uh-nul, all a-rig-uh-nul." Spirits began to sink.

Fritz had a contact from Intourist (a Russian service that provides guidance to tourists), and he bought three motorcycles for $2,500—a wartime Harley, a Matchless, and an Indian. The profits from the sales of the bikes would pay for the trip.

The rest of the time, "we went out and looked at junk, and cars that didn't exist. You know, a Russian would say, 'I know a woman whose brother-in-law's husband has a whatever,' and of course it didn't exist," Fritz said.

Two days later, Barry and Bud finally appeared. Bud, the man in Moscow, "turned out to be an arrogant sonovabitch," Fritz said.

"We said we'd like to see some cars, and Bud said, 'You can't just see cars. If you want to see cars, you gotta make an agreement that you're going to buy them now.' After a while, all we wanted to do was give him a nosebleed. Still, you don't close the door. We wanted to see the three cars in the photographs. And Bud said, 'Uh, no, we already sold those. They're already on the boat to America. You guys are just too late. If you don't move quick here, you don't get cars.'"

The Americans bit their tongues while Bud told them he had a Mercedes G4 six-wheeled car a thousand miles from Moscow inside a security fence at a Russian air base.

"We're just about at the point where we can get it. But we do have a Mercedes 770K W150 on a truck coming here, and there's a special four-wheel-drive Mercedes made for a German general, an open car," Bud told them.

Fritz told the story of the journey to see this:

"The next day, they take us to see this special Mercedes-Benz. They pick us up in this little junker. There are six of us packed into it like sardines. We get to an apartment, and they want one of us to go up, the rest to wait outside. So I give my money to my guys, and I go up. He begins telling me how this is all secret and 'we don't want anybody to know where we live' and where this and that is, and I say, 'Look, do you want to do something or not? We don't give a shit where you live, we don't care where the cars are, we don't know anything—just show us some cars, and we'll do something.' So we bring everybody up and we talk, and finally Bud said, 'Okay, I'll show you this car.'"

"So we drive twenty minutes away to a place where there are all these garage stalls. He opens up a padlock, and here's this Mercedes inside, the special car. Rich and I look at it, and Rich said to me, 'This is screwed.' He was right. It didn't have the right engine, or the right gearbox. Somebody had ripped the guts out of it and put in a four-wheel-drive truck suspension. So Bud said he's been studying the archives, uh-huh, and had reason to believe it belonged to General Zup-whatever and we could have it right now for thirty grand. Then he said, 'If you want to buy any of the other cars, you have to buy this one first, or I'm not going to sell you any of the other cars,' and we say, "Maybe we will, so what are the other cars?' And Bud said, "We have the 770K, but I need the money from this car to buy the 770K that's on the way here. I gotta pay the guy when it gets here.'"

That day was the last time they saw Barry and Bud. Then, just hours before the Americans were to leave for St. Petersburg, another contact named Stash appeared excitedly at their hotel at 10 p.m.

"He said he'd found some cars—a Mercedes 540K, a Mercedes-Benz roadster, and so forth," said Fritz. "So we run up and get our cameras, and we go to a guy's apartment who's an artist. He takes us to a garage with a dirt floor, and there are the cars—a nice white open car, a 540K, and a Horch. Wow! Rich opens the hood of the Horch and I see a blue-and white label under the hood. And I remembered it because I had looked at it under the microscope—in Barry and Bud's photos! These were the cars that were supposedly on the boat to America!"

The irony was that the proud owner was only too happy to show them off to visitors but had no intention of selling them. So Bud had simply photographed the cars and pretended he could deliver them.

They headed for St. Petersburg. Hearing that train compartments were more easily robbed than newspaper racks, the Americans locked themselves—and about forty grand—inside a compartment for the overnight trip. The trip was a bust, but they made more contacts. Ten days after arriving in Russia, they flew home, car-less.

Fritz was not discouraged. "Now we had all these guys in Russia working for us, looking for cars. This was just the start of business, and we knew we'd go back in a month or so. The cars are there. And big things were going to happen," he said.

In July, Fritz got a call from a woman who advertises for old Mercedes-Benzes in *Hemmings Motor News.*

"She said she got a call from this guy in Latvia," Fritz said, "and this guy's got a Mercedes 540K."

Fritz asked her, "What kind of 540K?"

"It's bulletproof," the woman replied.

With that, "my mind just took off," Fritz recalled. He eventually found an article in *Automobile Quarterly* on the 540Ks that Hitler had turned into armor-plated Aktion P cars for his inner circle. Pulse rates zoomed when he discovered that only one of those twenty was known to have survived, and it was esteemed enough to be in a Prague museum. So a second surviving car would be rare indeed.

The finder in Latvia was "Peter the Swede." Over the phone, he was asked to get the engine and chassis number of his find. The number he later gave was 408377, which matched one of the Aktion Ps that disappeared after the war. Now Fritz, Reuter, and Brewster wondered if Peter was simply reading back the *AQ* article to them. So Peter was asked questions that he could not have answered from a reading of the article—the thickness of the window glass, for example, which he didn't know.

Finally, Peter told Fritz, "You come over, and I'll show it to you."

He didn't have to ask twice. Four weeks after the first trip, the three Americans were back in Moscow.

And also back in the comedy zone. After a contact showed them an alleged "Stalin car"—this one a beat-up, bulletproof V-12 Packard—Fritz asked the owner, through an interpreter they'd hired, "How much?"

"Two million dollars."

"No, forget it; it's not worth two million dollars," Fritz replied.

The interpreter said something to the Russian, who made a counter offer.

"Okay, then, $250,000," the interpreter said.

"A helluva negotiator," said Fritz.

They went west after the Aktion P car. The train trip to the Latvian town took sixteen hours, with no food aboard. They were met at the station by Peter the Swede and a Latvian named Milan, who had put Peter on the trail of the Aktion P.

They all got into a car and drove deep into the countryside, finally arriving at a series of stone barns and houses. But the car's owner, a mechanic, was not there. When Peter was asked which barn the car was in, he sheepishly conceded that, well, he hadn't actually seen it, but, not to worry, Milan had—twelve or thirteen years earlier. The Americans rolled their eyes.

The mechanic's wife pointed out the right barn. Loose boards covering its doorway were removed. And then the Americans, having traveled all this way, found themselves face to face with a seven-foot-high pile of junk, scrap, and refuse. It looked as if someone had stood outside and tossed in every piece of junk that came his way during his lifetime.

"There's no car here," Reuter said glumly. Peter scampered over the junk pile and disappeared deep inside the barn. Finally, Fritz yelled at him. "Peter, is there a car in there?" Peter's hushed voice can be heard on the videotape: "Yeah. [Pause.] The body of a car."

Fritz said, "We climbed over, and there beneath the rubble we could see the top left portion of a roof and a left fender. We could see it was the right type body, and it was aluminum. And we knew we were onto something. The body was there, but it was in horrible condition. We looked inside and the armor plating was there, and we knew this was an Aktion P."

No one asked where the engine was, or inquired about the missing seats, or the wheels. They wanted to know just one thing: What was the engine and chassis number, and would it match a number on Daimler-Benz's official Aktion P list?

The frame was close by, buried under junk. Peter crawled down. The videotape shows him locating the stamped factory plate and rubbing it to reveal the numbers. Then you hear him reading it out: "Five-forty K. Four oh eight three seven seven."

Bingo. That Aktion P car was built in 1939 and assigned to the Third Reich's chancellery. Eva Braun may have taken a last ride in it. The diary of Martin Bormann, Hitler's secretary, said Braun took a "courier car" from the chancellery to Hitler's Berlin bunker on March 7, 1945, shortly before her suicide.

Fritz said, "We looked inside, and the armor plating was there and on the floor nearby. I looked at Rich, and our eyes said, 'Wow!' We tried to appear casual. What we wanted to do was shout. Finding it in that barn in all that junk was just incredible!"

Everyone piled excitedly into Milan's car and drove off to find the 540K's owner, whom we'll call Z. He lived an hour away in a duplex-sized building that was also home to three other families.

"We find him out in back, working on a VW, and we send Milan to talk to him. We're told this guy does nine different jobs just to get by, so we're expecting Milan to come back and say something like, 'Yeah, he said he'll take thirty-eight hundred bucks for the car.' But Milan comes back and said, 'He doesn't want to sell it.' What!? And Milan said, 'Not for any price.'"

"So he knows it's worth something, but we know it's worth more than what he thinks. So we drive back to where we're staying to try to figure out how we're going to get him to sell it," Fritz said.

They wondered if Z, a tall, pensive, bearded man in his forties, knew more about the car's value than he let on. Paranoia being what it is in his neck of the world, Z later told them he feared losing the car to the KGB or the Russian mafia. That's why he rented the barn space years ago, and spread out its many pieces in four barns, a puzzle that only he could put back together.

The job of wooing Z fell to Brewster, the wealthy, refined American who more than the others wanted the recognition that would come with this international discovery, this collector's coup. And why not? As the money man, he would pay.

So Fritz and Reuter went off in search of cars in St. Petersburg and Moscow, while Brewster, accompanied by a young interpreter named Mark, spent the evenings with Z and his family. But Z would not sell. A week later, the Americans flew home.

"Once in your life," Fritz said, "out of a thousand or a million cars, do you find a car in a barn that is this unique. We were not going to let this car go."

The phone calls to Latvia were regular, but Z didn't budge. He wouldn't sell.

"In the meantime," Fritz said, "Peter told us we could sell some American cars over there. So we sent over a Dodge Caravan and a Jeep and an '85 Mercedes-Benz 230 wagon that I couldn't make legal in America. We kept calling Peter and asking, 'Will he sell the P-car?' and the answer was always 'no.'"

In mid-September, Peter sensed that Z was weakening. Toward the end of the month, the Americans returned. Fritz laughs now at an idea they thought might win over Z.

"He had a daughter. We didn't see her, but somehow we thought she was nine. So, we thought we would get her some Barbie dolls, some nice toys—and a trip to Disney World for the family! And that first day, the daughter comes home, and she's not nine, she's sixteen. So there goes the idea. We work on the guy for a couple of days, and he said 'no' again."

Rich Reuter said, "It wasn't working. So we went to St. Petersburg to see some cars, and we left Brewster with Z. If any of us could pull it off, it was Brewster—he's relentless. He won't give up, but he's also quiet and polite, and they got along."

Fritz, Reuter, and their band of car hunters then got entangled with a volatile Russian who agreed to sell them a prewar Mercedes 170 Cabriolet A and three German Army Sahara R75 motorcycles. The Russian accepted $52,000 in cash, then reneged, disappearing briefly on delivery day. All this happened not too far from a place, Reuter recalled, where local thugs make sure everyone can see at least a portion of their shoulder-holstered handguns. Fritz went to the local cops, where the only reaction seemed to be their shock that anyone would be foolish enough to enter into a deal with this well-known gangster. Fritz finally confronted the welcher at his home and somehow got back Brewster's cash, but a good payday had been lost.

Returning to Latvia, they learned Brewster had been unsuccessful. They all felt that Z had been offered not just money, but something extraordinary. Then it struck them.

"We were told the daughter was an excellent student," Fritz said. But what future would she have in this emerging country?

"What if we offered his daughter an education in America? And along with that, and some cash, we'd also throw in the Mercedes-Benz wagon."

It was Tuesday, and Brewster would spend the next three nights massaging Z, leading up to that offer.

The Americans planned to fly to Finland, then home, on Friday. When Fritz went to bed Thursday night, he expected to leave empty-handed. He was awakened in the dark at 5:45 a.m. by an excited Brewster.

"Wake up, wake up! We got the car! We gave 'em an education for the daughter, the Mercedes wagon, and a lot of money." He was laughing. "Now, get up. You gotta figure how to get the car out of here!"

The obstacles seemed huge. The duty on this car would be determined by a local "expert"—in this case, the head of the local car club. But that man had made a small offer to Z for the car. Fritz said, "He'd know it was ours, and he'd say, 'Yeah, that's a twenty million–dollar car.' So we couldn't go the normal route. But we needed that customs stamp because we had to get it out properly. Z had proper ownership, and we had to go out of the country proper, and enter the U.S. proper."

Next, they called a man named Laszlo, whom they'd met in a run-down hotel—the only one near the local airport. Laszlo was the airport's air-traffic controller. Fritz asked him if he could hire a couple of planes. No problem, said Laszlo, except one—they couldn't be flown out of the country. He suggested Fritz rent them in Helsinki and fly them back.

"And any time you want the airport open, I'll open it for you," Laszlo said. "I can get you a customs man who will stamp anything."

For a small fee, of course.

Mark, the interpreter, called Finland and arranged for two planes.

"The problem," Fritz said, "is they weren't very big planes, but we got the cargo-bay measurements and figured we could get the car in if we cut off its roof."

They now believed that everybody and his dog in this suspicious little country knew about the car and the "rich Americans" poking around. It was not implausible that the Russian mafia would intercept them, taking the car at gunpoint or extorting a huge payment, or worse. (Reuter said of their entire time in Russia and the Baltics: "I wouldn't say we were nervous—I would say we were very nervous.") So the plan was to quietly collect all the Aktion P pieces over the weekend, and at precisely 2:30 Monday afternoon—an election that day would divert attention—bring in a rented flatbed truck, load it up, set off in convoy at dusk for the tiny airport three hours away, and then fly off under cover of darkness.

Suspicious of the phone lines, they bought a $2,300 mobile phone.

"There was a guy in the motel we thought was mafia," Fritz said, "and we didn't want to use their lines."

Meanwhile, Brewster took the phone and a new fax machine and went to a campsite in the woods that had electrical outlets. He then called the headmaster of his former prep school, seeking to enroll Z's daughter almost immediately. Brewster faxed the girl's school records. The school had accepted a lot of Brewster money, and it responded by finding her a place in a more appropriate New England prep school specializing in foreign students—children of ambassadors, foreign entrepreneurs—and she would soon be off to America.

On Saturday, Fritz and Reuter, using tin snips, gingerly cut off the car's roof along an existing seam. The engine block was dragged out by hand. The interior, which was stored in Z's mother's house, was brought to the barn. Hundreds of parts and body panels and armor plates were boxed up.

Laszlo, the air-traffic controller, was informed of their getaway time. He would open up the airport, no problem. And, Fritz asked, could he have a customs man on hand? "No problem," Laszlo said cheerfully. This part of the plan worried Fritz the most. If there was trouble, it would come at the airport. Who was mafia, and who was not?

On Sunday, Fritz took a hydrofoil across the Baltic Sea to Helsinki and "paid many thousands of dollars" for the plane rentals. "I told them they had to be there by ten p.m.—no later—and I said I wanted three seats on one of them because we're flying out with the car." He did not sleep well or long that night.

In the meantime, Milan let it slip to the local car club that the Americans were close to buying the car. Peter found out and warned Fritz. That almost guaranteed that the mafia would get wind of it. The anxiety level went up another notch. No one, including Z, was sleeping well.

Fritz returned from Finland on a commercial flight Monday morning. "We had nothing to do until 2:30, so we split up and drifted around town—in case anyone was watching us, they'd see nothing was up, and we were to meet back at two o'clock."

The flatbed appeared on time at the barns. But with it came two beat-up clunkers—a Fiat and some kind of panel van—as transport, and the Americans had one more thing to worry about. They carefully carried the body of the Aktion P into daylight and secured it on the truck. As planned, at 6:30 that evening they drove off in a convoy—Z in the flatbed, Peter and Rich in the Fiat, and Mark, Brewster, and Fritz in the van.

They drove on back roads. At an intersection, Mark's old van quit and wouldn't start.

"We jump out, and it's the cable connection to the battery. We prop it up, it starts, we get back in, and it stalls at the next stop.

We're very tense, and Mark—he's educated and well spoken, but he talks and talks in a roundabout way. Like he'd say, "It is said that, uh, in this area, uh, some 341 years ago—it may have been 345 years ago—that there was, uh, a particular carriage that was, uh, supposedly painted, uh, a bright, uh, yellow!"

We'd say, "Mark, shut up! Is the mafia gonna get us or what?"

After two hours on the road, the light began to fade, and fog moved in.

"Now we're worried the plane can't land," Fritz said. "We're not talking anymore. Then Mark said, really slowly, 'Well, it seems to my mind, there may be, uh, some floating sensation in the vehicle that I, uh, am able to detect in the steering wheel."

"Mark, whaddaya mean?" Fritz snapped.

"Well, I think there may be, uh, some difficulty with the inflation pressure of, uh one of the tires."

"Mark, do you have a flat tire?"

Risking being killed by the Russian mafia, smuggling suitcases stuffed with American cash, and offering to send the car owner's daughter to a New England prep school were some of the extraordinary measures needed to get the rare Mercedes out of Russia. *D. Randy Riggs*

"Yes; what should I do?"

"Pull over! Pull over!"

In the dark, five nervous men gathered around the van with the flat.

"Mark, where's the jack?"

"Well, you see, this had been, uh, a used vehicle, uh, when I purchased."

"There's no jack!"

The spare was buried under all the boxes, so it had to be removed. The jack from the flatbed did not fit. Finally, using a board, it was forced into place. Then they discovered there was no lug wrench.

"We got the lug wrench out of this Russian copy of a Fiat, and the van is I-don't-know-what, and I said, 'I'm going to make this fit. It's got to fit.' And it did!"

Back on the road, they were now running late. The fog became thicker.

"It got really quiet in that van. And Mark said, 'Well, it was quite fortunate that Rich, uh, mentioned to me to make certain that I, uh, check the, uh, air in the extra tire and wheel, which I had here, uh, in this vehicle."

"Uh-huh, and . . ."

"Yes, it was, because in fact when I checked it, uh, this morning, it was completely empty; it had no air."

"You mean the spare has a leak in it?"

"Yes, probably that's true, yes."

"Oh, wonderful."

"So, what do you, uh, suggest I do?"

"Drive faster!"

Shortly after 10 p.m., the silent, darkened airport appeared through the windshield.

"As we approach the gated entrance, this Russian guy comes out waving and yelling. Mark and he talk back and forth, and I say, 'Mark, what's going on?'"

"Well, you see, it seems the customs officer is, uh, not available."

"He's not available!?"

"Well, it seems, uh, that he lives quite close to here, but it's really, uh, within distance for him to walk."

"Mark, what're you saying?"

"Well, he's a young customs official, and as yet he does not have his own car and . . . "

"Mark, goddammit, you mean he needs a ride?"

Someone drove off to fetch him.

But now the Russian told them to drive around to a rear entrance to the airport. The rear? It was very dark, and the fear was now palpable. The convoy moved along the perimeter of the fence. Just as it arrived at an opening in the fence—whoomph!—a huge searchlight beamed onto the convoy.

"Oh my god!"

But it was only Laszlo, the air-traffic controller, lighting their way.

"Then I see the two Finnish planes," Fritz said. "The pilots are there, and they speak English. One of them said, 'You're late—we've got a problem. We have clearance for Russian air space, but only until 11:30.'

"So we had an hour and ten minutes to load all this stuff and distribute the weight equally between the two planes. I asked the pilot how we'd know if the weight was right, and he said, 'Well, if I take off and you're in the plane behind me and I crash, you know your plane will make it.' And then, out of the dark, twelve guys appear. Laszlo had found help to load the planes.

"I went in to see the customs guy. I sat in the little office, nervous, and he said, 'Here are the papers. It states you are shipping out this and that,' and then he stamps it. That's it; it's over. I give him a hundred dollars. And he said, 'Would it be possible that if I ever come to America you could extend an invitation [a visa requirement]?' And I just exhale, hard. "Sure,' I say. And I give him all the local cash I have, maybe twenty-eight bucks. So now we have the legal papers to export the car. And he said, 'Nobody ever checks these documents—they just throw them in a file.'"

By 11:15, the planes were loaded. Fritz distributed a lot of American cash to Peter, who would pay Mark and Milan. The Americans piled into the cargo bay of one plane. Brewster videotaped the takeoff. The tape shows Fritz opening a beer provided by the Finns, taking a deep swallow, then looking at the camera and saying, "This tastes really good." The plane lifted off, and three hours later they were in Helsinki.

The next day, they paid $7,000 to Finnish Air to ship them and the car by 747 to Kennedy airport in New York.

Editor's note. This article was reprinted with permission from the October 1996 issue of Car and Driver.

The Costa Rican Alfa Romeo

When I received an interesting e-mail from Carros Viejos in Costa Rica, I thought this was a person's name (I flunked high school Spanish). Had I paid better attention in class, I would have known that carros viejos means old cars in Spanish. The e-mail was from Franklin Rechnitzer, an old car enthusiast.

"I was in San Francisco last March and bought your book at the local bookstore," Rechnitzer wrote. "I think I may have a good story for your next book."

Rechnitzer has been an auto enthusiast since childhood, and owns several old cars. But the car that has been on his radar screen for decades evaded him until recently.

"One of the cars I own is a 1960 Alfa Romeo Spider 2000," he said. "It was bought new by my uncle, who bought it in Italy."

At the time, there were no Alfa Romeo dealerships in Costa Rica, so Rechnitzer's uncle had to have his new car shipped to the closest dealership—in Panama—and then he drove it to Costa Rica from there. This was in 1960, the same year his uncle's youngest son was born. This boy—Rechnitzer's cousin—grew up looking at the sports car and dreaming about driving it one day. That day came in 1975, when the boy was fifteen years old.

Forty years in the salty Costa Rican climate took its toll on the Alfa's metal bodywork. Franklin Rechnitzer waited patiently while the car his uncle purchased new in 1960 was passed on from family member to family member. In 2002, his chance to own the Alfa finally materialized. *Franklin Rechnitzer*

Rechnitzer's wife, Annette, initially not in favor of her husband purchasing another project car, saw the Alfa and fell in love with it. The couple's daughter, Anna, seems to feel the same. After restoration, Rechnitzer gave the car to Annette as a gift. *Franklin Rechnitzer*

"He didn't have a lot of driving experience, and he took the car without permission," Rechnitzer said. "Things went from bad to worse, and my cousin crashed the Alfa into a horse that had escaped from a nearby ranch!"

His uncle managed to have the car repaired locally, but the windshield had broken in the crash, and none were available locally. So the uncle parked the Alfa in his garage and promised never to sell it. Over the years, his uncle received numerous offers to buy the car, but the answer was always no.

In 2000, his uncle died and Rechnitzer's aunt inherited the car. Rechnitzer, who is thirty-five years old, also grew up admiring the car, so one day he made his aunt an offer to buy it.

"But my aunt told me that she had already sold it to her granddaughter's boyfriend," he said. "So I thought to myself, 'Well, I guess it was never meant to be mine anyway.' But two years later I met her granddaughter and she said that she and her boyfriend broke up one month after she agreed to sell him the car, so he hadn't paid for it."

Then the girl's mother decided to buy and restore the Alfa as a remembrance of her father. But then the mother went through a divorce, and had to sell her house and downsize to a condo. All during this time, the car was kept in a shed behind her house, and nobody had turned the engine over for many years. She knew that Rechnitzer was interested in the car and finally offered it to him.

Rechnitzer had another challenge, though. At the time he owned five old cars, and his wife didn't want him to buy another one. But Rechnitzer convinced her to take a ride to see the car before he cancelled the deal.

Instead of making her husband cancel the deal, she fell in love with the Alfa the instant she saw it. Eventually, Rechnitzer gave it to his wife as a gift.

"We are in the process of restoring the Alfa right now, and even though it is not as popular as the Giulietta model, I love it anyway," he said. "For me it has a lot of character and is kind of rare, being the only one in Costa Rica and one of just 3,443 built over four years."

Drag Comets in Paradise

BY TERRY HAMPSMIRE

My barn find started with a phone call from my brother, Gary. He was in the army, stationed in Honolulu, Hawaii. While he was there, I asked him to search the island junkyards for some "heater delete" parts for my 1965 GT350. Gary called late one night, and told me he had found something in one of the yards he visited.

"I found this car in the junkyard," Gary said.

"What kind?" I responded.

"A '65 Comet Cyclone."

"So? Did you forget where you are? How would you get it home?"

"Would you at least let me tell you about it?"

"Go ahead—it's your nickel."

"It's got fiberglass fenders, hood, doors, plexiglass windows, an altered wheelbase, a straight axle, five-spoke mags, and a parachute box."

I absorbed this for a minute.

"This is a joke, right? Very funny!" I said.

"No, I'm serious! What is it?" Gary responded.

"It sounds like one of the old A/FX drag cars. Get me some pictures, and any serial numbers you can find."

Gary sent me the pictures and the serial numbers. I couldn't believe what I saw. The big question, though, was whether it was one of the factory-built drag cars or privately built.

I called an old friend of mine in Oklahoma, Jim Wicks. Jim is widely known in the high-performance Ford community. If he couldn't help me, he would know who could. Jim called Rick Kirk, a fellow Oklahoman.

Rick owns one the finest original 1965 B/FX Cyclones in the country. He has collected serial numbers and data on a special breed of rare factory-built lightweight drag cars, the B/FX and A/FX Comets. He does not have a list of every serial number built, but the cars were built in batches, and he can tell if a number falls into a specific group or not.

The factory used several different FX classifications. Each class is decided by cubic inches-to-weight ratio. The FX stands for Factory Experimental. The Comets were classed as follows:

- A/FX: Big-block engine (427) and lightweight body.
- B/FX: Small-block engine (289) and lightweight body.
- C/FX: Small-block engine (289) and stock body.

All of the above had modified engines, with no horsepower restrictions.

Rick confirmed that the car my brother found could have been one of the Comet factory lightweights built by Bill Stroppe and Associates, in Long Beach, California. The serial number indicated the Comet was not an A/FX, it was a B/FX. The A/FX cars were given out by Ford to big-name drivers, while the B/FX cars were sold through the factory to anyone with enough cash to afford them. Both are rare, valuable cars.

Either was OK by me, as long as it was real. Gary went back to the junkyard to try to buy the car. The owner of the yard said it did not belong to him, but to a friend of his. He would not give the owner's name. He said the owner didn't want to sell.

Gary called me with the news.

"You're not leaving that rock without the car, so don't take no for an answer," I said.

He had to return to the yard several times before the guy finally gave in and told him where to find the owner. He immediately drove there, only to find it was true, he didn't want to sell. The owner had plans to return it to the drag strip. He also mentioned that someone from the mainland had contacted him about the car, but when he told them he would not arrange the shipping, they backed out. Apparently the cost of traveling to Hawaii and making all the arrangements was just too much.

After several conversations, the owner was finally convinced to sell the car. Gary borrowed a trailer from a friend and moved the car to a secure lockup area on the base. The next step was to answer the big question: How did the car get to Hawaii in the first place? The owner knew the history of the car, back to its original owner—Jimmy Pflueger, owner of Pflueger Lincoln-Mercury, in Honolulu.

The dealership was still in business, and still owned by Pflueger. Several calls were made to his office without making contact. Finally one evening, he called Gary at the base. Yes, he had owned the Comet. He bought it from Bill Stroppe, whom he had contracted to build the car. Stroppe had also built several engines for Pflueger's offshore race boat. Pflueger could not recall too much else about the car and suggested we contact the guy who drove it for him, Earle "Safari" Char.

Gary found Earle's name in the phone book. Earle invited Gary over to look at his scrapbooks. His wife had compiled several books with photos and newspaper clippings of race results. This proved to be a very important meeting. While looking at the pictures, Earle asked Gary, "Which Comet did you find?" Apparently, Gary had been referring to it, as a "Comet drag car," and hadn't mentioned the year.

It turns out that Pflueger had owned two Comet Cyclone drag cars. The first was a 1964 B/FX, which was white. It was powered by a 289 Hi-Po with Weber carburetors and a four-speed transmission. The second was a 1965 A/FX, which was red. It was powered by a 427 Medium Riser with Weber carburetors and a four-speed transmission. Both cars were built by Bill Stroppe and Associates. The 1965 A/FX was delivered to Hawaii with the standard wheelbase and no parachute. Stroppe removed the car's shock towers, added aluminum inner fenders, and installed straight axles. He also installed a Thunderbird-style hood scoop, although Earle has no idea why. It may have been to add enough clearance under the hood to accommodate the Weber carbs. Earle later altered the wheelbase of both cars and added parachutes.

Gary had found the 1965 A/FX, missing its powerplant. Despite the fact that the serial numbers indicated it was a B/FX, the information supplied by Earle indicated he had found one of the rarer A/FX Comets.

Rick believes that what happened was this: The 1965 B/FXs weren't selling as well as was anticipated. When Earle called Stroppe to order the A/FX, they decided to take one of the B/FXs and add the big-block engine and other goodies that made it an A/FX.

While the B/FXs were sold to the public, the A/FXs were not. Mercury Racing handpicked the drivers. They then sold them the cars for one dollar, with the stipulation they be returned to Mercury when the drivers were through racing them. Earle was not an established, big-name driver at the time, but Jimmy Pflueger had been an old customer. According to Earle, Pflueger paid $10,000 for the A/FX (using the Consumer Price Index, that would be about $57,000 in 2005 currency values).

At the end of their meeting, Earle told Gary that he might know where the 1964 B/FX was. He called Gary a week later, with the name of the current owner. He didn't know where to find him, but he was supposed to be racing the car. Gary went out to the drag strip a couple times, but there was no sign of him. He finally found a guy in the pits who remembered the car. He said it had been a few weeks since he had last seen the owner. The name he gave Gary matched what Earle had given him. The only thing he knew about him was that he worked in an auto parts store. Gary looked in the yellow pages for the store and found a whole chain of them on the island. He called shops until he found the one where the owner worked, but the man was off that day. He left a message for him to call, and after a week of waiting, he called again.

Yes, he had gotten the message, but had lost the number. Yes, the car was for sale. He had just pulled the engine out, and put it in his Camaro. He had been running a big-block Chevy in the Comet! (It was easier to find Chevy parts than Ford.) Gary found the

This photo is sure to increase the blood pressure of barn finders. Gary Hampsmire stumbled across this old drag Comet in a junkyard while stationed in Hawaii. Tramping down the tall weeds, Hampsmire discovered the car had fiberglass body parts, an altered wheelbase, and magnesium wheels. *Gary Hampsmire*

Comet sitting in the owner's driveway. They negotiated a price, and then closed the deal. Once again, Gary borrowed a trailer and moved the car to the base.

Prior to the purchase of the 1964 B/FX, we had already shipped the 1965 A/FX back to Illinois. Both cars were shipped by boat in sealed containers. The '65 A/FX was shipped to Los Angeles, then transferred to a truck, which brought it to my home in Illinois.

The B/FX was shipped to Los Angeles, as well. I happened to be in the state, so I drove to L.A. to pick up the 1964 B/FX. After securing the car on my trailer, I drove to Long Beach. There I located Bill Stroppe and Associates, still in business.

I spent a memorable afternoon with Stroppe. He told stories about his racing days with Parnelli Jones in *Big Oly*, the off-road Bronco. He had few recollections of any of the Comets they built, let alone ours. They were just a small part of the business that Mercury had contracted them to build. He did, however, recall his friendship with Pflueger, and how Pflueger asked him to build the '64 B/FX, and later the '65 A/FX. To the best of his recollection, the '64 B/FX was the only one they built.

One of the best-known 1964 B/FX Comets was campaigned by a well-known drag racer, Doug Nash. He built that one himself, from one of the Daytona endurance cars.

Earle told us he originally ordered the 1964 B/FX hoping to have it in time for the grand opening of Hawaii Raceway Park, which Mr. Pflueger was building. As opening day drew near, it became obvious that the car would not be completed in time. Earle was in contact with the head of Mercury Racing, Al Turner. During one of their conversations, Turner mentioned that "Dyno Don" Nicholson's 1964 Comet Wagon (*The Ugly Duckling*) was not being raced. Dyno Don had parked the wagon and started racing the two-door hardtop. They arranged to have the wagon shipped to Honolulu in time for the grand opening. All of Dyno Don's lettering was removed, and Earle had his name put on the roof.

If you compare the photos, you'll notice the decals on the rear side windows are the same. Of special note is the Crazy 8 decal, which was simply done by removing the "44." The wagon spent about three months in Hawaii, after which it was returned to the mainland and campaigned by "Fast Eddie" Shartman.

You may be wondering how Earle got his nickname "Safari." He says he and his friends used to travel to the other islands to go hunting. He referred to this as going on safari. It stuck with him throughout his life. Even today, his business is called Safari Auto Body. Earle "Safari" Char is somewhat of a legend in Hawaii drag racing circles. After racing both of the Cyclones, he moved on to race top-fuel dragsters.

Prior to going to work for Pflueger Lincoln-Mercury as a salesman, Earle worked at Castner Ford and raced a 1963 1/2 427 Lightweight Galaxie on weekends. The whereabouts of this car are unknown. It was rumored to have been destroyed, but it could still be out there waiting to be discovered.

A Crusade to Brooklyn

Curt Vogt was scared. He felt vulnerable as he sat up in the cab of the flatbed truck on a street in the worst neighborhood in Brooklyn, New York. After all, he was unarmed and had just given $10,000 in cash to a stranger.

He prayed the reward was worth the risk.

For a couple of years, Vogt had been following leads in pursuit of one of the most sought-after Mustang drag cars of the 1960s.

"I've always been a Ford guy," said Vogt, the owner of Cobra Automotive, a Shelby restoration business in Wallingford, Connecticut. "Even when I was a kid, I knew when I bought my first car, it was going to be a Mustang."

And so it was. Vogt turned seventeen in 1976 and bought a 1968 Shelby GT500KR convertible for $1,900 using money he earned mowing lawns, washing dishes, and doing other odd jobs. He sold the convertible in 1980, but the car left a mark on the young enthusiast. Since then, Vogt has owned somewhere between seventy-six and seventy-eight Shelby Mustangs—so many he isn't sure of the precise number.

One of the rare Holman-Moody–built A/FX Mustangs, pictured here in 1967 or 1968 when the car was driven by Jerry Harvey and Hubert Platt. The car, one of eleven built, was based on a stock Mustang fastback with unibody construction. *Curt Vogt Collection*

Under his photo in the 1977 Amity High School yearbook, this line was printed: "Baseball, hot dogs, apple pie and Ford—Death to Chevys!"

Vogt began buying and selling Ford high-performance cars after high school. He purchased his first Fairlane Thunderbolt for $350, a car that now sells for several hundred times that amount. He owned a lot of lightweight Galaxies, one purchased for just $450. But one car always represented the Holy Grail to Vogt. This was a car he would go to any lengths to own, including handing over ten grand to a total stranger in a bad neighborhood in the middle of Brooklyn. Vogt's Holy Grail was an A/FX Mustang drag car. He had tracked down and restored one. The prospect of a second was as irresistible as it was improbable.

This is an extremely rare factory-built race car, one of only eleven constructed in 1965. One was built as a prototype by Dearborn Tubing Company (the company that built Fairlane Thunderbolts under contract to Ford), and the remaining ten were built by Holman-Moody in Charlotte, North Carolina. These cars were constructed originally as K-Code (cars equipped with high-performance 289 engines) Mustangs. The cars were taken off the assembly line and had seventeen factory features removed. The parts left off included fenders, glass, bumpers, the engine, the transmission, and the radiator. The bodies were then shipped to Charlotte, where Holman-Moody installed 427-cubic-inch engines. Ford engineers had developed the single overhead cam (SOHC) 427 to combat Chrysler's Hemi in NASCAR. When NASCAR effectively banned Ford's new engine, the company decided to use it for drag racing. Holman-Moody could secure only seven of the 427 SOHC engines; the other three Mustangs received the high-rise 427 wedge.

These ten Mustangs, which had consecutive VIN numbers, were invoiced to either the dealer or the driver for one dollar each and shipped to drag racers throughout the United States. Gas Rhonda, Dick Brannon, Hubert Platt, and others all raced the new A/FX Mustangs, as did Len Richter, who raced out of Bill Stroppe's Long

Beach, California, shop. Richter's A/FX (VIN 5FO9K380237) was the second car built by Holman-Moody. It was originally painted Poppy Red, but repainted Champagne Gold for Richter's sponsor, Bob Ford.

Richter entered the car in the 1965 Winternationals, racing his way right up to the finals, where he faced off against the Tasca Ford. His Mustang's axle broke, and victory went to the Tasca car. All during that season, the Mustang's wheels, although remaining stock in dimensions, were pushed forward in relation to the body in order to aid traction by placing the engine's weight closer to the rear axle.

After the 1965 season, and some rules changes in A/FX, Mustang No. 2 was sent back to Charlotte, where Holman-Moody converted it to a 1966 model by placing the wheels back in their original location, then replacing the grille, quarter panels, and other trim items. The car also received a 1966 Holman-Moody ID tag.

After Richter drove it, Jerry Harvey and Hubert Platt raced the Mustang before it was sold to "Dyno Don" Nicholson for the 1969 season. By this time, the four-year-old race car was getting a little long-in-the-tooth as it competed against new cars such as Sox and Martin's Hemi Dart. Still, Nicholson continued to win. The last time Nicholson drove the Mustang was in 1969 at Englishtown, New Jersey. Dyno Don popped the clutch at 9,000 rpms and made it

Even though his car was in its racing twilight years, "Dyno" Don Nicholson (standing in yellow T-shirt) was still competitive in 1969, beating the new Hemi Dodge Dart of Sox and Martin, among others. This photo was taken at the NHRA Grand Nationals in Indianapolis. *Curt Vogt Collection*

through the traps at 9.89 seconds, setting a new NHRA track record and winning the class for the season.

By the time Nicholson steered the Mustang back to the paddock, men with bags of money were waiting for him. They wanted to buy the car, and they offered him so much money that he couldn't say no.

In the 1960s, there was a strong connection between street drag racers, numbers runners, and drug dealers in the New York area. These dealers took in lots of money—all cash—and needed to find places to spend it. A guy named Tab bought the car from Nicholson and raced it on New York's Connecting Highways and other stretches of straight asphalt against GM and Mopar teams. Rumor has it that Tab would wager as much as $150,000 on a single run. It is said that the Mustang won more than $1 million in one summer from one Chevy team alone!

Eventually, though, the car disappeared.

Curt Vogt was selling telephone systems in 1988, when he heard that Dyno Don's old steed might still exist in the New York area. He had already found and restored another of the eleven original A/FX Mustangs—one that Al Joniec converted to a stretched-nose Funny Car and campaigned as the "Bat car." Vogt savored the thought of another A/FX car—less than fifty miles from his Connecticut home—but he doubted the rumors were true.

"I'd go to all the local swap meets and I'd talk to guys who said they knew the old Nicholson Mustang was somewhere in New York City," Vogt said. "But I really didn't pay attention because I knew that Nicholson drove Mercurys. Little did I know that he drove this Mustang between his time in Pro-Stock and the Funny Cars."

"When I found out that Nicholson did in fact race a Mustang, I called every speed shop and machine shop in New York City, Brooklyn, Queens, Long Island, and the tri-state area."

Then, one day out of the blue, Vogt got a call from a boisterous Mustang collector named Drake who said, "Hey, I know where the old Nicholson car is in New York City, but you'll never find it!"

Gold metal flake paint long gone, the once-beautiful drag car fell on hard times when it was nearly forgotten in a Brooklyn storage garage. Gone was the 427 single overhead cam drivetrain, but the Holman-Moody ID tag and front magnesium wheels were still in place. *Curt Vogt*

"He was bragging and overly confident," Vogt said. "He just knew he'd wind up with the car eventually. I begged him, but when he wouldn't tell me, I stepped up my quest to find the car myself."

Phone call after phone call led to dead ends, but then Vogt had a chance conversation with Long Island engine builder, Jack Merkel. Merkel said the Mustang sounded familiar, and thought he remembered someone named Lucky once painted the car for a guy named Tab.

Finally, a lead!

Tab was a numbers runner and a drug dealer who was apparently bumped off—dead. But rumors of his death were greatly exaggerated, because he was still alive. But he no longer owned the car. Tab sold it to someone named Tex.

More phone calls revealed a guy named Lucky, who owned an independent towing business in Queens.

"Yeah, I know where it's at," Lucky told Vogt.

"I was on him like a tick," Vogt said. "I dug in and I wouldn't let go. I must have called him two hundred and fifty times over the course of the next year. It took me fifteen months from the time I started looking for the Mustang until I finally had a shot at buying the car."

Vogt hooked onto Lucky, and through him met his friends Jessie, Three Notes, and Rags. Lucky found Tex, the sixty-year-old-

Vogt displays the Mustang's parachute, which was still folded up and stuffed in the back of the car. *Curt Vogt*

street-savvy guy who now owned the Mustang. Tex worked on cars in a dark, dirty one-bay garage and in the street off Myrtle Avenue in Brooklyn.

"I offered Lucky five thousand dollars in cash as a finder's fee," Vogt said. "And I kept fifteen to twenty thousand with me at all times in anticipation of getting a phone call that this car would become available."

"One day he called me and said, 'I think we can buy the car.' I drove to Queens and met at Lucky's apartment.

"I left my pistol at home."

Vogt climbed into Lucky's flatbed truck. Vogt gave Lucky $10,000 in cash. On the way to Brooklyn, they picked up Lucky's friend Bob. Vogt was sweating bullets. He had just handed over a large amount of cash to a stranger, and he was headed for a bad neighborhood and had no idea what would happen next.

"They could have rolled me," Vogt said.

The trio pulled up to Tex's repair shop, and Lucky went inside to try to negotiate a deal. Vogt stayed outside in the truck and talked to Bob.

"He was cool," Vogt said. "He told me a lot of street racing stories."

These negotiations took a couple of hours. Lucky came back out to the truck and said, "Tex said he won't sell the car."

"I gave Lucky another couple of grand, but despite Tex's needy-financial condition, he didn't want to sell; it was a no-go," Vogt said.

Frustrated, Vogt drove back home to Connecticut. He was so close to buying a car he had chased for so many months, yet so far away.

Then, two weeks later, on June 13, it was ninety-six degrees outside, and Lucky called to report that Tex had changed his mind.

Vogt jumped into his car and hightailed it to Queens. He and Lucky jumped into Lucky's flatbed, and they drove toward Myrtle Avenue, just the two of them.

"It was a real bad area," Vogt said.

When they arrived in Tex's neighborhood, Lucky jumped out of the truck and went in search of Tex. Vogt stayed in the truck. He stuck out like a sore thumb, so he slumped way down in his seat and tried to disappear.

After about a half-hour, Lucky returned to the truck without the money. He told Vogt they need to drive a few blocks away to pick up the car, which he now owned for $11,000, purchased sight unseen. They drove to a garage in a desolate area. Tex opened the garage, and there, in the rear of the dusty garage, sat a gray primered Mustang sitting way up in the front, complete with its Holman-Moody ID tag still mounted.

"I had finally found the Holy Grail," Vogt said. "We pushed it into the daylight. It still had its four-inch-wide American racing magnesium front wheels and a parachute with the Ford logo on it."

Lucky and Vogt pushed the Mustang out of the garage and onto Lucky's flatbed, but before they could leave with their booty, they had to pay homage to Tex and his friends in Tex's speakeasy, an after-hours nightclub that he ran up one flight of stairs and down a narrow hallway. The club contained some broken-down pool tables and pinball machines. The two fulfilled their social obligations and left as soon as they could.

Lucky was proud; he showed off the car all over Brooklyn, finally stopping at a speed shop to show his buddies the long-forgotten Mustang.

After a lengthy restoration, the ex–Don Nicholson A/FX Mustang is once again in pristine condition as it sits in Vogt's Cobra Automotive shop. Vogt regrets selling the car in order to buy a 427 Cobra, but he is again on the trail of a similar Mustang. *Curt Vogt*

"I was like a celebrity," Vogt said. "I was in with all the brothers."

Lucky delivered the car to Vogt's house in Connecticut and collected his $5,000. "We unloaded the car in my driveway, shook hands, and said goodbye."

Vogt eventually had the Mustang's body restored by the Super Stang Shop in Lyons, New York, but he supplied the 427 SOHC and drivetrain from his own business, Cobra Automotive.

Having had his fun with the car, and wanting to acquire another car of his dreams (a 427 Cobra), Vogt sold the Mustang A/FX in 1991. He has regretted it ever since.

But he recently received an e-mail from a friend who said he knows a guy whose son bought a 1965 Holman-Moody drag Mustang for $1,200 in the late 1960s.

Maybe it's time for Curt Vogt to pack a briefcase full of cash and find a fresh cast of characters in a shady part of town.

The Incredible Disappearing Chevelle

Franklin Rechnitzer remembers the first time he saw the 1967 Chevelle 396 like it was yesterday.

"It was in 1987 and I was seventeen years old and in my first year of college," said Rechnitzer, now a doctor. "Even though I remember seeing this car cruising on the boulevard, at the time I did not know what kind of car it was."

Chevelles are rare in Costa Rica, where Rechnitzer lives. He has always loved cars—his Alfa Romeo is described earlier in this chapter. Today he has a small car collection, but when he was in college, and immediately following graduation, money was tight. Still, the car was special, and he hoped to own it, sooner or later.

The 396-cubic-inch 325-horsepower Chevelle was originally bought in the United States by the owner of a movie theater as a surprise gift to his wife. But when it finally arrived in Costa Rica, she decided the Marina Blue metallic Powerglide automatic car with its bucket seats was not her style, so she seldom drove it. Instead, the big-block Chevy was parked in the lot of the movie theater, where it remained for three or four years. The intense sun took a toll on the car's paint job.

Eventually, the Chevelle was sold to a doctor who used it regularly until the fuel crisis hit in the early 1970s. At that time, the car took another sabbatical, sitting at the doctor's office for nearly fourteen years. In 1984, a young auto mechanic approached the doctor, who had retired, and offered to trade his late-model Toyota for the old blue Chevy. He knew what a Chevelle was and was pleased when the doctor accepted the deal.

Rechnitzer first saw the car with the young mechanic at the wheel. He was a student in his first year of college and remembers seeing the mechanic/owner driving the car on the main boulevard in the capital city of San Jose.

"This was where the guys used to drag race, but I never remember seeing this car racing or being hammered," he said. "It really amazed

The car that Franklin Rechnitzer chased for so long. Even though the paint was poor, all the sheet metal was original and sound. The car's third owner was Luis Fioravanti. The woman pictured is Luis' wife.
Franklin Rechnitzer

me that this guy never, never raced the car, even though his friends pushed him to do it. Years later, I found out that he truly cherished the car and the engine and did not want to overhaul it."

Although he was entranced by the blue car's lines and projection of power, Rechnitzer did not even know what kind of car the Chevelle was because they were so rare in Costa Rica. He poured over hot rod magazines in search of an answer. But the car got away from him. Rechnitzer later met a friend of the mechanic, who told him that the mechanic had gotten married and his wife had a baby. His priorities had shifted, and he had sold the car.

In 1997, Rechnitzer was a newly graduated doctor. Costa Rica requires its new doctors to work as general practitioners in the rural countryside for one year after graduation. Even though the pay for this work is low, Rechnitzer managed to save enough money for an old car.

One weekend, he went back home to visit his parents, when—surprise—he discovered the blue Chevelle parked at a used car lot

With a fresh coat of paint, a rebuilt 396 drivetrain, and new wheels, Rechnitzer's Chevelle would look good at any Saturday night American cruise-in. His daughter Anna certainly seems to think so. *Franklin Rechnitzer*

just two blocks from his parent's house. Unfortunately, this was Sunday afternoon, and, as luck would have it, the car lot was closed. Rechnitzer had to leave that evening for his rural medical job.

"So, I asked my dad to go see about the Chevelle the next morning," he said. "I even called him at 7 a.m., but he forgot to go. The car was sold that day.

"I told myself that maybe the car was not meant for me, and just forgot about it."

Two months later, Rechnitzer was again visiting his parents in San Jose. During that trip, he bumped into a car-guy friend of his. In fact, Rechnitzer had helped this guy restore a 1957 Chevy Belair that had been a basket case. The friend mentioned that he had just bought a blue 1967 Chevelle. Rechnitzer almost fainted. The car had been parked because the engine had excessive smoke coming from its tailpipe. The 396 V-8 was ready for a rebuild.

This friend mentioned that he was getting married and wanted to sell one of his cars: the '57 Chevy or the Chevelle. Rechnitzer jumped at the offer to buy the Chevelle, but his friend wanted him to buy the '57 because of all the hard work he had put into it when they restored the car. So he bought his second choice, the '57 Chevy.

The friend's plans were to use the money from the sale of the '57 Chevy to buy things for his new house and also to invest in the restoration of the Chevelle, Rechnitzer said. "But as time went on, he used all the money on the house and none on the Chevelle, so again it was put in hibernation in the garage. I eventually lost track of him, and he wound up selling the car to a muscle car enthusiast."

Five years later, in 2002, Rechnitzer was living in San Jose and still owned the '57 Chevy and a '55 Chevy one-ton truck. He had a chance conversation with his former friend who sold the Chevelle from under him.

"I told him I thought it was incredible that he never offered me the Chevelle when he decided to sell it," Rechnitzer said.

Feeling bad, his friend mentioned that he had heard a rumor that the new owner of the Chevelle wanted to sell it, and if he was interested, they could go visit him. It took several hours to locate the Chevelle owner's house, but eventually they met with the owner and found out the rumor was true; the Chevelle was for sale.

The Chevelle's engine and transmission had been overhauled, but its paint and interior were in poor condition. The owner had all the receipts for the overhaul expenses in a folder, and he offered the car to Rechnitzer for that amount plus a little bit more. They agreed on a price, but the sale was far from over.

In Costa Rica, a car can only be sold if it is fully operational and approved for use on public roads. Rechnitzer said the national vehicle bureau is very tough on older cars. The problem was that the windshield was cracked, and to pass the inspection, this would have to be fixed. The owner received an estimate of $350 and agreed to pay for the new glass. But when the final bill came in at almost $1,000, the owner could not afford that much money. He was planning to buy a 1984 Corvette and needed all the money for that purchase. Additionally, the owner's brother, who was trying to talk him out of selling the car, called and informed Rechnitzer that the deal was off; the car was no longer for sale.

Again, Rechnitzer was convinced this car was not meant to be his.

Two days later, the owner called Rechnitzer and told him that if he agreed to pay the difference for the windshield, he would agree to sell the Chevelle.

Rechnitzer agreed.

On the day the sale took place, the owner brought his brother along. The brother tried to convince him not to sell the car—that if he did, one day soon he would regret it. Rechnitzer tried his best to ignore the brother's ranting as he completed the transaction.

After years of admiring and attempting to purchase the Chevelle, the car was finally Rechnitzer's. He restored the car and is pleased with the overall results. Even though the paint was lousy, the sheet metal was all original, except for the left front fender, which had probably been replaced by the first owner.

One year after acquiring the Chevelle, the old owner called Rechnitzer and wanted to buy it back.

"The Corvette was not the car he had hoped for," Rechnitzer said. "He kept the car in a clear plastic bubble and never drove it. He only drove it about thirty-five miles since he bought it."

The owner admitted he had made a mistake and wanted the Chevelle back.

"I told him that I had waited for this car for almost twenty years, and it was going to be real hard to get it away from me," Rechnitzer said. The Chevelle was meant to be his after all.

CHAPTER TWO

The Find Next Door

They're Under Your Nose

BY BILL WARNER, FOUNDER AND CHAIRMAN OF THE AMELIA ISLAND CONCOURS D'ELEGANCE

I am often asked, "Where do you find all those neat cars?" Most of the cars I have found, particularly those featured in *The Cobra in the Barn*, turned up within three hundred miles of my home in Jacksonville. Since the last book, I've discovered and bought two more interesting cars. One is a Buick Landau, a rather unusual sedan built by the Buick Division for the 1954 General Motors Motorama. The other is a 1926 Chevrolet race car, known as the

Built for the 1954 Motorama show, this 23,000-mile Buick Landau survived the crusher. Bill Warner first saw the car offered on eBay, then in *Hemmings Motor News*. The car was ignored by other collectors; only Warner realized its significance. *Bill Warner*

Simplex Piston Ring Special, which, for the past eighty years, had been less than ten miles from where I live. In both cases, I was tipped off about the cars by car-guy friends. I am also restoring a Maserati Ghibli that I purchased in the 1980s.

I learned of the Buick through a telephone conversation with Rick Zeiger, who lives in Los Angeles and collects classic cars as well as rare postwar Cadillacs—El Dorado Broughams, to be exact. I told him that I had always wanted a Motorama car and had chased several over a period of more than thirty years, but had never landed one. He mentioned that a Buick Landau was currently on eBay, and although he found it interesting, he had too many projects to take on and was going to pass on it. I logged on and there she was. There was a $55,000 reserve on it, and no one had bid. I watched it closely, but hesitated to open the bidding. The auction ended as a no-sale. The following week, my *Hemmings Motor News* arrived, where the same car was listed for $75,000. Other than a Skylark, there are very

Surviving for more than eighty years in a garage just ten miles from Bill Warner's Jacksonville, Florida, home, this Chevrolet beach racer was called to Warner's attention by an acquaintance from California. It was purchased from the family of the original builder and driver, Bert Moyer. *Bill Warner*

few 1954 Buicks worth $75,000—but this one was different; it was a real life Motorama show car. My phone call connected me to the owner, a woman who acquired the rare Buick in a divorce settlement.

I made an offer sight unseen—except for photos—and she accepted in July 2004. Once the car arrived in Jacksonville, I solicited help from Randy Kimberly, who had recently retired as the area service guru for General Motors. We commenced an on-chassis restoration on what was basically a sound, 23,000-mile car. It had survived the crusher after its service on the show circuit by serving as General Motors VIP transportation in Detroit and New York City. It had since passed through four owners, including Del DeReese (one of the first board members of the Meadow Brook Concours) and Atlanta's Mark Hamburger.

The car had some rocker panel rust, and the right rear bumper tip was rotted out. Other than that, it was in fair shape. About the only things missing were the shot glasses and cocktail shaker from the fold-down armrest and the unique turbine hub caps. Our target was to have the car ready for Don Sommer's Meadow Brook Concours in August 2005.

The race was on to get the one-off Landau ready for Meadow Brook, and after many sweaty days, and help from Amelia Island Concours Board Member David Leedy, we made the show by stuffing the car into the FedEx/Passport truck only days before the event with the interior door handles and some final detailing yet to finish. The car arrived in Detroit and we took it to Steve Pasteiner's Advanced Automotive Technologies in Auburn Hills to finish it for the Sunday show.

This significant and interesting show car was right under everybody's nose—advertised on eBay and in *Hemmings*—yet nobody moved on it. The trick was recognizing something important and stepping up to the bar. The lesson here is to be a student of the automobile and stay on top of all forms of media that list cars for sale.

Maserati Spyder

Another car now boarding at Chez Warner was a Maserati Ghibli Spyder, also under my nose. The car belonged to my banker's father, who had bought it from the late Peter Gregg in 1970. Gregg had used the Maserati at his estate in Ireland and later in Jacksonville. But the car had seriously overheated in the warm summer traffic in Jacksonville, after which the 4.7-liter Maserati V-8 was replaced with a small-block Chevy. The car had resided in my banker's father's garage untouched for about ten years.

In about 1985, my banker asked me to give him an estimate on restoring the car, which was basically sound with exception of the engine swap and some Bondo in the right front fender. I estimated the restoration would run between $55,000 and $70,000. After a month or so of mulling, he called and asked if I wanted the car. The unrestored price was less than five figures, and the next day it was mine. I have just started the restoration and through the kindness of John Weinberger at Continental Autosports in Hinsdale, Illinois, I have the correct engine. Hopefully, the car will be finished within a year and my wife, Jane, and I can enjoy a great luxo-cruiser. The lesson here is that even your friends may have interesting cars stuffed away.

Chevy Race Car

In October 2006, I received a call from Alan Taylor, the renowned restorer in San Diego, asking me to check out an early Chevrolet racer in Jacksonville. Now I was really perplexed as to how a car could have escaped my attention in my hometown. Here was Alan in San Diego telling me about this racer less than ten miles from me. Boy, was I off my game. I felt that after over sixty years in Jax, I knew every weird or significant car in town, and to have someone three thousand miles away tell me about it really shot my automotive ego in the differential.

A call to Sally Moyer revealed that she had a Chevrolet race car built by her father-in-law in 1926 to race on the beach at Daytona. After a twenty-minute drive to her house, I found the car as advertised—in pieces, mind you, but all there. The simple and crude bodywork was good only for patterns, but the car was complete.

Her father-in-law, Bert Moyer, had raced it at Daytona, Ormond, Ponte Vedra, Pablo (now Jacksonville Beach), and Brunswick beaches, as well as Camp Foster (now the U.S. naval air

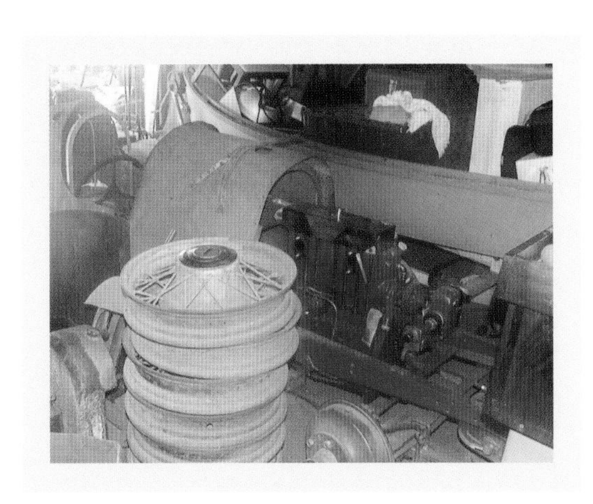

Based on 1926 Chevrolet mechanicals, the car competed in races in Daytona, Ormond Beach, Ponte Vedra, and Lakewood Speedway in Atlanta. Moyer began to restore the car in the early 1960s, but passed away before its completion. Included in the sale were scrapbooks, race records, and photos. *Bill Warner*

Restored just in time for the 2007 Amelia Island Concours d'Elegance, Warner's find attracted several General Motors executives, who said that it may be the oldest Chevy race car on the planet. *Bill Warner*

station in Jacksonville) and the Lakewood Speedway (Atlanta) from 1926 until 1932. He started the restoration in the early 1960s, but passed away before he could finish it. In short, the car had been in the same family for eighty years.

Additionally, Sally had all the photos, negatives, newspaper clippings, programs, pit passes, ribbons, cloth helmet, and letters surrounding the car and her father-in-law's racing career. Wow!!! The paperwork and records were fabulous. The car is now in my shop. Randy Kimberly and I restored it and unveiled it at the 2007 Amelia Island Concours d'Elegance. This extraordinary find shows that there are worthy cars virtually in your backyard—even if the only person who knows about them lives across the country. Don't feel that you will have to find your dream in some far off corner of the world. It may be as close as the next block over.

A Cunningham in the Neighborhood

When Vail Frost saw an ad for a Cunningham in the Chicago Sunday paper back in 1975, it piqued his curiosity; he had no idea what a Cunningham was.

"I was a car nut, so I read the antique car section of the classifieds every Sunday," said Frost, now the owner of a commercial landscape company in Alpharetta, Georgia. "I said to myself, 'I've never seen one,' so I didn't set out to buy it."

From the prefix on the telephone number, Frost realized the advertiser was in the same suburban Chicago neighborhood where he lived, so he called and took the one-and-a-half block walk to see this car called Cunningham.

When he got to the home, he met owner Dave Dubel. A racing accident at the wheel of a Mercedes 300SL had left Dubel a quadriplegic, but he was still an avid car collector. Although Dubel had

When Vail Frost purchased the Cunningham in 1975 in his Chicago neighborhood, its restoration had already begun. The seller, a quadriplegic man, had painted the car white with blue stripes, the traditional American racing colors of the Cunningham team cars. *Vail Frost*

purchased the Cunningham to restore, he had since decided to concentrate on 1930s classics.

What Frost found was not a complete car, but a basket case. Yet it was reasonably priced, so he bought it.

"If you've ever bought anything disassembled and tried to put it together without instructions, you know what I was up against," Frost said.

Original builder Briggs Cunningham didn't have it much easier. Cunningham was intent on winning the 24 Hours of Le Mans with an American-built car and American drivers. He built his race cars in the unlikely location of West Palm Beach, Florida. Initially Cunningham's cars were Cadillac powered, but the Caddy engines eventually gave way to Chrysler's powerful new Hemi.

Cunningham's challenge was this: To race at Le Mans, his cars had to be homologated—that is, racing versions of production street cars. Cunningham's race cars weren't derived from a production model, so he had to work backwards and build one.

Cunningham built his street model—the C3—alongside his racers in Florida, but buyers didn't exactly line up to purchase the king-size sports car. In 1952, a C3 coupe sold for $9,000, significantly more than Ferraris, Maseratis, or other prestigious sports cars of the day. In reality, though, the wealthy Mr. Cunningham never planned to profit from these street versions; he only wanted to comply with the Le Mans rule makers. Making Phil Walters, one

Frost immediately began stripping the paint, which revealed lots of Bondo and bad bodywork. Business and moves began to infringe on Frost's restoration efforts, and ultimately the car went into a thirty-seven-year hibernation before he rediscovered it in his garage. *Vail Frost*

The huge sports car's secret lay under the hood: a 331-cubic-inch Chrysler Hemi engine topped with four two-barrel carburetors that produced nearly 300 horsepower. *Vail Frost*

of his lead drivers, the sales manager for the production car further shows that Cunningham had other priorities than selling C3s to the general public.

After the chassis were fabricated in Florida, they were shipped to Italy, where Vignale produced the Michelotti-designed bodies. The cars were then sent back to Florida for finishing. Even though exact production numbers were never documented, evidence suggests that twenty coupes and between four and nine cabriolets were built.

Frost's coupe, the fourth built, left the factory with a gray-and-blue paint scheme and was originally purchased by Edmund du Pont.

Now that he owned a car that just days earlier he hadn't even heard of, Frost didn't know where to begin.

The car's interior and glass had already been stripped out, but the 331-cubic-inch Hemi engine, manufactured by Chrysler's industrial division, was complete and correct, as was the fluid-drive semi-automatic transmission. From what Frost could tell, the major missing pieces were the seat and bumpers. He searched out and documented parts for several months until he was transferred to North Carolina.

The car was boxed up and moved to his garage in Asheville, where it sat for the next several decades.

One day he discovered a barn find . . . in his own garage.

"The car was collecting dust when my wife said I'd be dead before getting around to fixing that car up," he said. "So I spent a

Finally, in 2004, Vail Frost and his wife, Linda, proudly displayed their pride and joy on the lawn at the Amelia Island Concours d'Elegance, where it won the Most Outstanding Hemi award. Restoration of the Vignale-bodied car was completed by White Post Restorations. *Frost Family Collection*

lot of time investigating restoration shops before deciding on White Post Restorations in Virginia."

Finally, in 2002, after thirty years in his hands, Frost's Cunningham was headed for restoration. He borrowed a seat from another Cunningham owner in Vermont, and had a duplicate fabricated. Interestingly, because of the car's width, the Continental Coupe is equipped with a three-passenger bench seat.

"You don't realize how huge the car is until you park it next to a similar vintage Ferrari," he said.

The Cunningham's restoration took two years—from January 2002 to January 2004. Upon its completion, Frost was invited to display the car at the Amelia Island Concours d'Elegance, where it won the Most Outstanding Hemi award from *Super Rod* magazine.

After thirty years, the double barn-find Cunningham was finally seeing the light of day.

The Divorcee Cobra

Word was getting out. One day in 1997, one of Brian Barnes' clients—a gentleman named Delbert—said to him, "I heard you bought a Cobra."

Barnes was thinking, "Oh, boy, here it comes; he's going to tell me that I make too much money."

But instead Delbert told him that his daughter had two Cobras parked in her garage—and that she and her husband hadn't driven them in twenty-five years.

Barnes thought this couldn't be true; surely these cars must be some sort of Mustang II decal package or at best a special-edition Torino.

"Tell your daughter to call me if she ever wants to sell them," Barnes said to Delbert. Several months went by when Barnes received a phone call late one Friday night.

"This is Delbert's daughter," said a lady's voice. "Sorry it has taken so long to respond, but I've been out of town for a while. But yes, I would be interested in selling the Cobra."

Barnes still didn't believe this could be true, so he asked for the car's VIN number. Delbert's daughter asked Barnes to please hold on while she went to retrieve the car's title. She returned to the phone and said "CSX . . ."

The hair on the back of Barnes' neck stood on end. ". . . Two, three, one, seven," she continued.

Barnes was stunned as he ran across the room to grab his Shelby American World Registry to check the car's history. It read: "Vineyard Green w/ beige interior; shipped with Class A accessories, white side wall tires and no luggage rack, plus antifreeze, $5,449.05. Sold through Town & Country Motors in Reseda, California. No ownership records since 1972."

Barnes was in shock. "Can I come over to see them in the morning?" he asked

"Sure," she said.

Like in a dream, Brian Barnes followed up a lead that he knew must be wrong—two forgotten Cobras in a garage—and found out the story was true. The Cobras had been parked for twenty-five years. *Brian Barnes*

Barnes had a hard time sleeping that night. He showed up on her doorstep at 8 a.m. He wasn't prepared for what he saw next. She brought him into the garage, turned on the lights, and showed him four cars under covers. Under the first cover was a Ferrari 308 GTB with only eight hundred miles on the odometer. The second cover's unveiling revealed a red 427 Cobra, which had not seen the light of day since 1976. The woman explained that she had been through a divorce. In the settlement, she received the small-engine Cobra, and her ex-husband was awarded the large-engine Cobra. The third cover concealed the 289 Cobra, which had only 22,000 miles on the odometer. Under the fourth cover was a Sunbeam Tiger. The woman explained that another car, a GT350, had just been sold.

The two Cobras had been sitting for so long that the tires were flat and the brakes were frozen.

Barnes stayed looking at the cars and talking to the woman for at least an hour. She told him that she and her ex-husband had purchased the 289 Cobra in 1972 for $4,500.

Although neglected, the 289 Cobra was incredibly sound. It was so original that the factory crayon markings behind the radiator for chassis No. CSX 2317, normally worn off with time, were still very much intact. Barnes purchased the car for $75,000, even though the owner wanted less. *Brian Barnes*

Because he already owned a 289 Cobra, CSX 2242, Barnes was not in a position to purchase the woman's Cobra.

"My wife and I had just recently bought a Cobra, and she was not very keen on me buying another one," he said. "We were broke."

"So I offered to get the Cobra running and help her sell it."

"My wife knew, though, that once I got the car home in my garage, I would want to keep it. She wouldn't even go with me a few weeks later when I picked it up with a flatbed."

Barnes couldn't loosen the brakes, so the Cobra had to be dragged by chain onto the flatbed truck.

Once he got the car home and surveyed its condition, he calculated how much work and money would be required to get CSX 2317 running again; he called the woman a week later. Barnes told her that in his estimation, it would take about seventy-five hours—which he would donate at no charge—and about $7,000 in parts.

"At the time, small-block Cobras were selling for about $125,000," he said. "She wanted me to buy the car, and asked if I would give her $70,000 for it. I told her that amount was way too little. She said $75,000 was her final offer.

"The car was the last link to her ex-husband, and she wanted to end that connection."

Also forgotten in the garage was this 427 Cobra, a Ferrari, and a Sunbeam Tiger. At the time Barnes bought the 289 Cobra, the other cars were not available for purchase. He now has an urge to see if they might still be parked there. *Brian Barnes*

Better still, the woman offered to hold the note on the Cobra for two years at 8 percent interest. So Barnes worked overtime at his mortgage banking business and had the debt paid off in just six months.

When he began inspecting the Cobra, he realized that this was a pretty special car. The car had been painted by Shelby's painter, Tweedie, in a deep blue-purple-black. Tweedie also installed fender flairs before the car was delivered to the first owner. The Cobra was so untouched that the original crayon CSX 2317 markings scrawled on the car by factory workers were still on the chassis behind the radiator.

"Tweedie remembered the car and remembers painting it," Barnes said.

The car is equipped with pin-drive hubs and Halibrand wheels. CSX 2317 also has Ballinger headers and an engine that Barnes believes was built to Stage IV Comp specs. It has modified heads and a high-lift cam. And because the original owner had plans to race the car in SCCA competition, he also had Shelby install a roll bar.

"It was like the original owner went through the Shelby parts catalogue and ordered all sorts of parts," Barnes said.

The engine had been sitting for a quarter of a century, so before firing it up, Barnes soaked the cylinders with Marvel Mystery Oil. When he cranked and fired the engine, it filled the neighborhood with smoke. But it ran perfectly.

Despite his original plans to sell the Cobra, Barnes kept the car and still owns it today. He sold his other Cobra, CSX 2242, to a friend. He has kept CSX 2317 mostly original, replacing only the mouse-eaten interior and some of the wiring harness, which had also been damaged by rodents.

"I've probably driven twenty-five small-block Cobras in my life, and this is the tightest one I've ever driven," he said.

So what ever happened to the other cars in the garage?

"I don't know," Barnes said. "For all I know, they are still sitting there.

"Hmmm . . . I think I'll give her a call."

Officer Barn Find

Matt Mercer has the perfect job. While most of us drive past barns, garages, and outbuildings wondering what might be inside, Mercer has a more legitimate reason to venture onto private property than the rest of us.

Mercer is a police officer near Boston, Massachusetts.

"Whenever I respond to a call, I can't help but take a look in the garage to see what might be hibernating in there," he said.

Mercer's interest in old cars predates his entering the force.

"I've always been fascinated by old cars that have sat unused and neglected, so I began riding around neighboring towns on my moped when I was too young to drive," he said. "I'd peek into backyards and garages and quickly discovered that if you take the initiative to bang on a door and ask a few questions, you may get more than you've bargained for."

Using this method, Mercer has scored himself some nice trophies. Even though he regrets never stumbling across a Cobra, or an

Officer Matt Mercer is always on the look out . . . for interesting cars. Here is the 1961 Lincoln Continental convertible, complete with suicide rear doors, that he considers his ultimate discovery. He purchased the car from the estate of the deceased owner. *Matt Mercer*

Parked for thirty years, the Lincoln was a "steal" at just $1,500. Mercer confirms that "barn finds are alive and well." *Matt Mercer*

interesting race car, he did purchase a 1971 Chevelle coupe with only 30,000 miles on it from the estate of the original owner for only a thousand dollars in 1987. He still owns it. He also became the owner of a 1975 Ford F-250 truck with only 29,000 miles, which he received for free; a 1975 Dodge Coronet with 25,000 miles that he bought for $400; and a 1985 Ford F-250 with only 9,700 original miles.

More recently Mercer heard about a barn on a huge estate that was formerly owned by a car collector. Officer Mercer contacted the attorney handling the estate and asked if he could take a look inside the barn. Inside were a Packard convertible, a Studebaker convertible, a 1950s vintage Jeep, and an early 1960s Lincoln suicide-door sedan. These cars had been parked thirty years ago and were in amazing condition, but they weren't for sale.

"I lost many nights sleep thinking of these dust-covered time capsules," Mercer said.

Mercer also stumbled upon a 1967 Pontiac GTO convertible, equipped with a 400 cubic-inch engine and a four-speed transmission. The car's eccentric owner allowed Mercer into the garage to see the car, which hadn't moved in twenty years, but again, the car was not for sale.

About two years ago, Mercer stumbled across another find, a 1961 Lincoln convertible that had been sitting in the garage of an elderly woman for more than thirty years. She told him that she didn't want the car, but it wasn't for sale.

Under a cover next to the Lincoln sat this 11,000-mile 1961 Rolls-Royce Silver Cloud. The car was purchased new in Boston and driven sparingly until being recently purchased by Bill Payne of Fort Mill, South Carolina, who will use the car in his limousine business. *Matt Mercer*

"She told me to contact her estate upon her passing," he said. "She passed away a few months ago, and I began an attempt to contact her heirs."

Mercer dropped off several letters at the estate and was finally contacted by an attorney, with whom he negotiated a price of only $1,500 for the Lincoln.

"This car was my personal Holy Grail, one that I had been searching for forever," he said. He bought it even though he had never actually been inside the garage and seen the car under the cover. And there was a second car he viewed through the window in the stall beside the Lincoln. . . . "Before her passing, the lady told me that she also had an old Rolls-Royce, but didn't elaborate on the year or model," Mercer said.

It turns out the Rolls was a 1961 Silver Cloud that had been sitting for at least three decades. Mercer said that the eleven-thousand-mile car appeared to be rust-free and that the interior was beautiful, but some mildew needed to be removed. The estate's executor recently sold the car for $15,000.

Because of his lucky finds, Mercer wants to leave car collectors an encouraging message: "Barn finds are alive and well. All the cars I've found were within the parameters of one small town where I patrol."

And Matt Mercer's career might just be the next-best barn-finding advantage to having x-ray vision!

The Author's Barn Finds

Hunting for old cars is what gets me up in the morning. Since I was twelve years old, it's been my passion. I have the good fortune of traveling a fair amount in my career, always carving out enough free time to go "looking for sheds," as we used to call them.

Below are a few of my personal barn-find stories; some are recent and some are from a number of years ago.

1963 Abarth Monomille Coupe

Clearly Jim Dana was not ready to die. He had so many automotive and airplane projects underway that he could have easily used another decade to get them all completed. But complications from a heart attack in 2001 ended an incredible automotive journey.

I never met Jim Dana, but I feel I know him well. As a teenager and young man, I passed his house and was always treated to cool cars parked in his driveway. A Porsche Turbo, a Lamborghini Countach, and a Pantera. I also remember odd little Italian cars—Abarths—that seemed to frequent his home in Long Island's suburbs. I remember that the small sign in front of the house told me that he was a doctor, and that he kept an office in his home. But the interesting vehicles in the driveway told me he was a car guy.

Years passed, decades actually, and after thirty years of living on Long Island, I moved to Charlotte, North Carolina, to pursue a career in NASCAR marketing and public relations. Occasionally, though, I'd visit relatives back in my old hometown during business trips. Riding around in my rental car on one of these trips in 2006, I decided to see if the interesting cars on Brown's Road near Nesconset Highway were still there.

As I approached the house, I thought, "This is insane; to imagine that the same person still lives here since the 1970s is wishful thinking." But there, through the window in the garage door, I could see an engine hoist.

"Could it be?" I wondered.

I parked the car in the driveway, walked to the front door, and rang the doorbell.

A woman answered the door, carrying one small child in her arms with another following close behind.

"Excuse me," I said, "but I remember some neat cars parked in the driveway about thirty years ago. Does a car guy still live here?"

The woman looked somewhat surprised.

"Well, no, a car guy doesn't live here anymore, but a car person lives here," she said. "My husband died five years ago, but I like cars, and I still have most of his collection. Come in, I'll show you."

This is how I met Alice Dana, Jim Dana's widow.

She was babysitting her grandchildren, who were obviously having a great time at Granny's house. In the middle of keeping the kids entertained, she explained that her husband was a car and flying enthusiast who left many projects unfinished.

"He was a brilliant doctor, but his heart was in the garage or the hangar, modifying cars or building airplanes," she said.

Alice had only just decided to sell off Jim's cars and parts—until that point, it would have been too painful to see them go.

We walked down to the basement garage to see his piles of Porsche, Fiat, Ferrari, VW, and MG parts, mostly new and obviously left over from earlier projects. Jim Dana also had quite a machine shop, complete with a CNC machine, a Bridgeport milling machine, lathes, and welders. Many Mazda and Moto Guzzi engines littered the shop, along with a mid-1980s Lotus Esprit. I found out that in his latter years, Jim did most of his fabricating at an airplane hangar he owned about twenty-five miles east in the town of Shirley.

We took a ride out to the hangar and saw a number of experimental airplanes and a few cars, including a two-cylinder Fiat 500, one stock and one very modified Porsche Turbo, an MGTF, and a home-built Moto Guzzi–powered trike. But it was the Abarth that caught my attention.

It was a 1963 Monomille aluminum-bodied coupe. (*Mono* in Italian means one, for single cam, and *mille* means one thousand, which refers to the engine displacement of one thousand cubic centimeters.) I had always liked the Abarth designs when I saw them in the vintage racing paddocks. They had a definite sports car look. But to me, the low roofline and nearly horizontal back window gave it the appearance of a chopped 1950 Mercury—something that customizer George Barris might have had his hand in creating.

This would be a fun car to own and restore. But there would be challenges.

Alice told me that the car had not been driven since 1967 or before, and even though it had only twenty-five thousand miles on it, the engine was frozen due to its long hibernation. Jim had also begun to modify the aluminum body to resemble the more racing-oriented twin-cam Bialbero coupe with its slanted, more aerodynamic headlights and front cooling vent.

Alice told me that of all the cars Jim owned, this one meant the most to him. As a college student, he admired the accomplishments

I remember this car from my youth, sitting in a driveway usually filled with other interesting cars. Little did I know that one day, nearly forty years later, I'd own it! The Abarth Monomille was built for hillclimbs, but driven to medical school by original owner Jim Dana. *Tom Cotter*

of builder Carlo Abarth and the cars he manufactured and modified out of his shops in Torino, Italy. He followed the racing successes of the Abarths and decided that one day he would own one. That day came in 1962, when Jim placed his order directly to the Abarth factory for a 1963 Monomille Coupe, modified for hillclimbs. The agreed price was $3,015. During college break, Jim and his older brother Tom traveled to Torino to see the car being constructed.

Once the car was completed and shipped to New York, Jim used the Abarth to commute to medical school in New York City. When he and Alice were married and lived on Staten Island, the Abarth, along with a Fiat 500, became their family cars. He drove the car with gusto, and he had at least one fender-bender with it before parking it when other cars came into his life.

"But he never wanted to sell the car; it always had a special place in Jim's heart. I knew this would be the toughest car for me to sell," she said as she fought back tears.

We agreed on a price quickly; she was asking $12,000, I offered her $10,000 and we settled at $11,000. A fair price, I thought, for a one-owner, unusual car with an interesting history and full documentation.

When I arrived a couple of weeks later to pick up the car for its seven hundred-mile trip back to North Carolina, it was pouring rain. Many areas around Long Island were flooded as it rained nearly four inches in just a few hours. As I installed the ramps on my trailer, Alice told me that she had cried most of the morning, hoping she was doing what Jim would want.

"I'm thinking that he's angry, and that all this rain is his way of telling me that," she said.

But then she confided in me that she believed when I knocked on her door that morning a few weeks earlier that I had been sent from heaven.

"I'm very rarely home, and the fact that you came walking up, found me at home, and asked about the cars was a sign that Jim was still looking out for me," she said.

Dana began to modify the body, but became involved in other projects and simply parked the car. His widow, Alice, was pleased to sell her late husband's car to someone who had remembered the car for several decades. *Tom Cotter*

As my son Brian and I finished securing the Abarth on the trailer, and tried to stay dry, Alice took photos and video images, and said goodbye to the car that for so long had been a part of her life, too.

As we drove away from the hanger that morning, the rain stopped and the sun peeked out.

Jim was happy.

1967 Shelby Mustang GT500

"I'll have one cheeseburger, an order of fries, and a Shelby Mustang to go, please."

It wasn't quite like that, but a cheeseburger and a plate of pancakes actually did help my friend Jim Maxwell and me purchase a 1967 Shelby Mustang GT500 from the person we thought was the original owner.

Bob Ramsuer was an ocassional road racer back in the 1960s and 1970s. A colorful character, he raced an Austin-Healey 3000 before stepping up to a 1966 Shelby GT350. A bad wreck in that car brought his driving career to a halt. But all during this time, Bob operated a little luncheonette in the North Carolina town of Lincolnton. Bob's restaurant, which closed for good around Thanksgiving 2006 because he was getting tired, was famous with locals who would come, eat, and listen to Bob give his opinion on nearly any subject.

Most of those locals didn't know that Bob still owned a unique car, even though the walls of the diner were festooned with photos of Bob's road racing exploits. After all, he drove a Dodge minivan; surely his car days were over.

Not quite.

I met Bob when I worked at Charlotte Motor Speedway. I was one of a handful of people who knew that behind a small vacant house that Bob owned a few blocks away, sitting without a cover, was a GT500. I had never actually seen the car, but on occasion, Bob mentioned to me that he owned the special Mustang and that people were always bugging him to buy it.

I had first heard about the car in the mid-1980s, when GT500s weren't the hot collector cars they are today. Then, about ten years later, I purchased an old NASCAR stock car from Bob's son, Stuart, who was broke and hanging up his helmet on a once-hopeful NASCAR career.

When Bob Ramsuer finally decided to sell his wife's Shelby GT500, I'm glad he chose me and my friend Jim Maxwell as its new owners. The car sat in this backyard for decades and was well known by collectors, but nobody ever made Bob a fair offer. *Tom Cotter*

"How's that Shelby doing, Bob?" I asked as I purchased the rough old stock car.

"It's just sitting there in the yard," he said.

"Want to sell it?" I asked.

"Nope!"

So I stored that car away in my memory bank for another decade.

Finally, after selling the 289 Cobra chronicled in *The Cobra in the Barn* at the 2005 RM Auction in Monterey, my friend Jim and I were hot to find another Shelby barn find.

"You know," I said to Jim, "I'll bet old Bob Ramsuer still has that GT500 he's told me about for so long. I haven't ever seen it, but he's a good guy, and I don't think he's pulling my leg."

So I drove forty-five minutes to Lincolnton for breakfast one morning.

"Tom, what the heck are you doing here?" yelled Bob from behind the lunch counter. "How many years has it been?"

Knowing that Bob was a Ford racing fan, I presented him with a copy of the Holman-Moody book that I wrote several years ago, then I ordered breakfast.

"I thought you'd like to have this," I said, and then asked if he still had the Shelby.

"Yup" is all he said.

I didn't say anything more.

About a week later, I went back to Bob's diner for lunch. I ordered a cheeseburger and fries. This time Bob came out to my booth and sat with me. We spoke for a while about his racing photos on the wall.

"Tom, I really appreciate the book," he said. "Say, you're always asking about the Shelby. Would you like to see it?"

"Oh yeah," I said.

Within minutes, I was a passenger in his minivan as we apexed turns in the neighborhood just a few blocks away. In the yard behind a small brick house sat the sorry-looking lime gold Shelby, covered with leaves and pine needles, looking forgotten.

Bob unlocked the door. I sat inside. The seats had mildewed, but the car was surprisingly correct and complete. And it only had thirty-four thousand miles on the odometer. The automatic-equipped car was like a time capsule; even the exhaust system was original. So were the heater hoses and all the clamps. In fact, the original tags on the carburetor and the distributor were still in place.

"Want to hear it run?" Bob asked.

I had to catch my breath; you mean to say that a car that has been off the road since 1980 still runs?

"I had a mechanic buddy of mine go through it and get it running," he said. Clearly he had given thought to selling the car, and I just happened to be in the right place at the right time.

Fortunately, that mechanic didn't remove the original parts, as is often done with restored collector cars.

Bob jumped behind the wheel, and she fired right up. The car ran well, although loudly, because time and corrosion were parting out the original exhaust system.

As the car sat there idling, Bob told me the story of buying the car from Hickory Ford in North Carolina for his wife to drive to her job at the real estate office. That's why it had an automatic. And that's why I believed he bought it new.

Odds were good that since it was his wife's car, it was not driven as hard as a typical "guy-owned" muscle car would have been back in the 1970s.

He asked me how much I'd offer him for the car. I said I'd like to come back the next week with Jim, look the car over really closely, and then be prepared to make an offer.

Jim is a nut for originality. The following week we came armed with Jim's parts books and combed over the car. It was real, it was low mileage, and it was possibly one of the most-original Shelbys in existence. Even the original Goodyear Sports Car Special spare tire was still in the trunk, probably still inflated with the original 1967 air.

At left: The decal on the trunk lid displays the long-gone Shelby Owners Association. Below: Open the trunk and one of the original Goodyear Power Cushion tires is still mounted as a spare.
Jim Maxwell

But first, we ordered cheeseburgers and fries from Bob's diner.

Making an offer was going to be tricky business. Sure, we would like to own the car for the least amount of money possible, but I didn't want to low-ball Bob, who had become a friend. I'm sure that the scores of other folks who hounded him over the years tried to "steal" it.

We came up with a fair market value of the car of $65,000; not free, but it was an amount we thought both Bob and we could live with.

"Boys, you just bought yourself a car!" he said.

The following week, when we went to retrieve our new acquisition, Bob had discovered two more of the original tires that came on the car, and proudly presented them to us.

We had the car looked over by Walt Pierce of Huntersville, North Carolina, who specializes in maintaining original Ford performance cars. He tuned the car, rebuilt the brake hydraulics, and changed all the fluids. The Shelby runs great, although still loudly because we refuse to change the original exhaust system.

We drove the GT500 to the Shelby National Convention at Virginia International Raceway during the summer of 2006 and it was a hit. There, among hundreds of beautifully restored Shelbys and Cobras, sat our GT500 rat, and boy, did people love it. Judges combed over the car looking for the multitude of untouched details that every Shelby came with new.

"Please, never restore this car" was a theme Jim and I heard over and over. "Save it as a reference for all the other restored '67 GT500s."

Since that time, the car has been displayed at Lowe's Motor Speedway at AutoFair, next to several restored Shelbys to highlight the newly introduced GT500. Craig Jackson, of the Barrett-Jackson Auction, was at AutoFair that week appraising cars for a television special that would air before his 2007 auction.

Craig loved the car.

"Don't restore this car," he said.

It seemed that we really had a unique set of wheels on our hands.

While at AutoFair, a gentleman named Jim Adams introduced himself and said that he had actually purchased the lime gold Shelby new in 1967.

"I worked in the dealership body shop, and a customer ordered this car," he said. "But when the car came in, the customer decided he didn't want it. So I bought it and owned it for two years. When I sold it, it only had 1,200 miles on it."

How did Adams identify the car?

"The car came without stripes, so I painted those black stripes right in the dealership body shop. I could tell my stripes anywhere."

Datsun 510

I've always been a road racing fan. My first racer was a Datsun 510, an inexpensive car manufactured from 1968 to 1973. The Datsun 510 featured an incredible number of standard features—independent rear suspension, overhead cam engine, disc brakes—that rivaled more expensive models from BMW and Alfa Romeo.

In order to gain exposure for its attractive 510, Datsun contracted with racers Pete Brock and Bob Sharp to transform cars into SCCA racers. Brock prepared cars for the 2.5 Liter Trans-Am class, while Sharp modified 510s for B-Sedan competition. Suddenly every road racer on a tight budget could aspire to own an economical road racing or hot street car.

I was one of them.

I bought my 510 for $250 back in 1977. It was mildly modified, but slightly damaged. Once repaired, this car became a dual-purpose vehicle for me, street-driven during the week, raced at road circuits like Bridgehampton, Lime Rock, and Summit Point on the weekends. But when I moved from Long Island to Charlotte in 1985,

In its heyday, my old 510 was competitive in Eastern Motor Racing Association races at circuits like Bridgehampton, Lime Rock, Summit Point, and Bryar Motorsports Park. It was also my daily driver. *Tom Cotter Collection*

Looking somewhat forlorn, the old 510 was sitting in Ronnie Clifton's side yard in Winston-Salem, North Carolina, just fifty miles from my house and six hundred miles from where I sold the car. *Tom Cotter*

I sold the car to friend and fellow 510 racer Mario Birardi of Flemington, New Jersey. And even though I had really enjoyed 510s, I basically forgot about the car. Until about twenty-five years later.

One day I received a phone call from Ronnie Clifton of Winston-Salem, North Carolina. Turns out he was a friend of Mario's, and he told me that he owned my old 510 race car!

"Mario owned the car for about ten years, then gave it to me," Ronnie said. "It's been in my backyard for about fifteen years. You are welcome to come and pick it up for free if you want it."

Wow, what luck! What I discovered, though, was a very rusty and mostly dismantled car. Yet my tape stripes and signature Foster's Beer oil recovery can were still in place; how could I say no? So I trailered the car home and hope to one day restore it to the street/track car I owned so many years ago. I have since collected many of the suspension and drivetrain components that were originally on the car, and I only seek the time to dig into the project.

Graham Hill's Lotus Elan Series III Coupe

My wife Pat and I were attending an Austin-Healey convention in the mountains of North Carolina. We stayed in a quaint little bed and breakfast. In the morning we were treated to fresh blueberry muffins, juice, and a copy of the Sunday *Asheville (North Carolina) Citizen* newspaper. As all good car guys know,

The way the Lotus Elan looked in my garage for the ten years I owned it. It was as though I had a barn find in my own garage! Lotus driver Graham Hill received this car when he was named driver on the Lotus F1 team. *Tom Cotter*

the first area of the newspaper to check is the antique and classic ads in the classified section.

Wow, there were three listings: a Ford Model A and two Lotuses—a late-model Esprit and a '67 Elan. The Elan really got my attention because the ad read, "Originally owned by Graham Hill."

Huh? How did Graham Hill's Elan wind up in the North Carolina mountains?

It turns out that both Hill and teammate Jimmy Clark received Elan street cars as gifts in 1967 for driving for the Lotus F1 team. I even secured a photo of Hill smiling as he received the keys to his new ride from a London Lotus distributor.

When Hill eventually tired of the car, he sold it to a gentleman who brought the Elan to the United States. After a few years, the car was sold to "Chris" of Long Island, who drove the car to college, then to Maine, then North Carolina, where he settled in the town of Brevard and opened a cabinet shop.

When I responded to the ad, I was invited to Chris's cabinet shop, where I found the depressing sight of a nearly totally disassembled Elan coupe covered in sawdust.

When he showed me documentation of Hill's ownership, I committed to buy the car for the advertised price of $6,500 and gave him a deposit. Word got out about the car, however, and the next day Chris called me and said I still had first rights to buy the

Looking splendid in its original yellow paint, my old Lotus Elan was originally presented to two-time F1 World Driving Champion Graham Hill (left) by London Lotus dealer Ian Walker. How the car ended up in a cabinet shop in North Carolina is a long and interesting story.
Tom Cotter Collection

Lotus, but now the price was $10,000 because a collector in Chicago had just offered him that amount.

Hmm. A deal is a deal where I'm from, but it seems a few thousand dollars were more important to the seller than his word. Nonetheless, I agreed to the higher price, and I picked up the car and all the parts the next week. I dragged the car home, put it in the garage, and didn't touch it for a decade.

I always seemed to be involved in another project that interested me more. For a while, I considered converting the coupe into a vintage race car, but my friend Peter Egan talked me out of that idea because Hill never raced the car. He only street drove it; modifying it would ruin its heritage.

At one point during my ownership, I was contacted by Graham Nearn, owner of Caterham Cars, the continuation builder of the famed Lotus 7. Nearn desired the car and offered to trade one of his Caterham 7s for the basket case coupe, but I said no. My justification was that I could always own a Caterham, but only one person could have Graham Hill's Elan.

But after ten years of doing nothing with it, I decided to sell the car to someone who would appreciate the project more than I did. I advertised it in *Thoroughbred & Classic Cars* magazine in England and ultimately sold the car to a Graham Hill fan in England for $10,000—just what I had paid ten years earlier.

Wish I had that one back.

CHAPTER THREE

Rare Finds

The Superbird in the Bushes

Barry Lee first heard about the Superbird from an unreliable source. After all, the guy had already snookered Lee out of two Plymouth 'Cudas that he had pursued on eBay.

"This guy would deal in muscle cars," said Lee, a motorcycle dealer near Jacksonville, Florida. "But he sold the two 'Cudas from under me after I had committed to them."

Lee's business was booming, and this allowed him to pursue the Mopar muscle cars he had loved since he was a kid. He was into Chrysler's big-block 'Cudas, Super Bees, and Challengers. But his dream was to someday own either a long-snouted, big-winged Plymouth Superbird or its similarly styled cousin, the Dodge Daytona.

These cars were built with one purpose in mind: to win NASCAR races. The slippery nose and tall tail helped these cars go fast and stay planted, earning wins for drivers such as Richard

Find the hidden Superbird! At first, Barry Lee didn't see the Superbird he had heard about in an Alabama yard. It had been parked behind a house for nearly thirty years, and eventually the hedge grew up around it. *Barry Lee*

Petty, Buddy Baker, and Bobby Allison. But the street versions were never winners in the showroom. The odd-looking vehicles were sold to the public for homologation purposes only; NASCAR rules required that a certain number of street versions be built for any model a manufacturer wanted to race on the stock car circuit.

Lee's not-so-dependable contact must have had a change of heart, because he phoned Lee to tell him about a Superbird he heard about in Alabama.

"He told me something about the car having been owned by a guy who was missing in action in Vietnam, and it had been sitting since 1975," said Lee. "He gave me an address and only asked for a finder's fee if I purchased the car."

Fair enough, Lee thought, and he made plans to see the winged Plymouth.

"Alabama was more than four hours from my home, and my wife wasn't in the mood to take a long drive," he said. "But I told her I'd take her to Biloxi, Mississippi, for some gambling over Christmas if we could stop in Alabama on the way. She was all for it."

When Lee pulled up to the house, he thought the wheeler-dealer Mopar salesman had pulled another fast one on him. The property was overgrown, the house was abandoned, and the roof had collapsed. Lee walked around the yard and looked at a couple of old trucks and cars that were lying about, but there was nothing exciting. Then his wife noticed a small piece of bright orange inside the hedge. Lee pushed away the branches and discovered the car of his dreams: a 1970 Plymouth Superbird that had actually become part of the hedge!

Lee found out who owned the house and called the phone number.

"When I called and asked about the car, they hung up the phone on me," he said.

The elderly owner, Frank Moran, whose wife was in a nursing home, lived nearby with his daughter.

"So then I had my wife call, and she and Frank were having a nice conversation until she mentioned the Plymouth. Then he hung up on her too."

Even though the car had only thirty-five hundred miles on it, all those years parked in the salty, humid air near the Alabama coast certainly took its toll on the rare Plymouth. According to Lee, nearly every metal panel needs repair or replacement. *Barry Lee*

As Lee pulled away the hedge to get a closer look at the Superbird, he discovered just how trapped the car was with vegetation that had grown up around it. *Barry Lee*

The Lees went on to Biloxi and had an enjoyable holiday, and decided to pursue the Superbird later.

Lee gives his wife full credit for coming up with a plan on acquiring the Plymouth. Call it woman's intuition, but she suggested that they simply write a letter that expressed their desire to buy the car. What did he have to lose?

It was several weeks after their Alabama trip that Lee wrote the letter to both the elderly Frank Moran and his daughter. In it, he said he'd like to restore the car—to remove it from the elements that were destroying it—and that Moran could keep the title. It was quite a charitable offer, but it went unanswered.

"It was out of my hands," Lee said. And at least a year went by before he received a surprise phone call.

"Hello, Barry? This is George Proux, Frank Moran's son-in-law," the caller announced. Lee's heart began racing. "Frank fell and is in the hospital. I have power-of-attorney, and I had all the cars hauled off before I found your letter. I figured I should give you a call and let you know that the Plymouth you are interested in is sitting at my house in Jacksonville, Florida."

Only about fifteen minutes from Lee's house!

Proux was a muscle car enthusiast. In fact, when he first married Moran's daughter, he had tried to purchase the Superbird from Moran, but he was denied. With Moran's declining health, Proux and his son hauled the car to their Florida home in the hopes of restoring it. But Lee hoped they would consider selling it, because the Superbird's restoration was more than an average hobby restorer could handle.

Proux said that a museum in Alabama had been calling about acquiring the car, but he wanted to give Lee the first opportunity because the letter he had written was so sincere.

"I went over and looked at the car and we talked," Lee said. "At the time I was driving a very nice, 1970 factory big-block lime green Road Runner."

Lee and Proux traded.

"He got what he wanted and I got what I wanted," said Lee, very pleased with the transaction.

Lee's barn find is equipped with a numbers-matching 440-cubic-inch engine, column-mounted automatic transmission, and bench seat. It still has its original bias-ply Goodyear Wide Oval tires mounted on rally wheels. It was one of 1,920 Superbirds manufactured.

It was only after he acquired the car that Lee was finally able to meet Frank Moran and learn of the car's history.

"Frank was a super-nice guy; he was in a walker when I met him," Lee said.

Moran had traded a boat for the Superbird in 1974. He drove it, but didn't enjoy being followed by people who wanted to talk to him about the car. Apparently, Moran once ran off someone inquiring about the car with a shotgun.

"He was kind of a private guy," Lee said.

Parked in a barn near Lee's house in Jacksonville, Florida, the car reveals its rough condition. Even the firewall has cancer. Yet Lee looks forward to the ultimate restoration, which he will begin immediately after his two other projects. *Bill Warner*

Finally, having driven it less than one thousand miles and fed up with the notoriety the car was bringing him, he pulled the car out of sight and parked it behind his house. Eventually the hedge slowly engulfed the orange car so that it wasn't visible even to someone standing next to it. That's where Lee first spotted the car. Unfortunately, the time since he first saw the car had taken its toll on the Superbird's condition.

A hurricane that took landfall in Pensacola in 2004 blew down a tree, which broke out the back window and dented the roof and rear quarter panel. Then thieves had made off with many of the car's unique parts, such as the rear wing, hood, radio, front fender scoops, and radiator.

"I was surprised at the car's poor condition when I saw it in Jacksonville," he said.

Luckily, Lee came across a "clone" Superbird, from which he was able to buy replacements for many of the stolen metal and fiberglass pieces. However, he still needed the rear window—which is unique to the Superbird and extremely rare. Incredibly, Lee was able to locate a parts vendor in Myrtle Beach, South Carolina, who had a brand new rear window for the car still in the original carton.

"I finally have my dream car," Lee said. "This car is a keeper."

"It will get a full rotisserie restoration and be the most serious restoration I've ever done. Because of the moist, salty, and humid environment the car had lived in for so many years, the floors, trunk, frame rails, and some of the firewall need to be replaced."

But first, Lee is completing the restoration of a 1969 Super Bee. Then a 1969 Camaro Convertible. Then a 1971 'Cuda.

Then comes the Superbird.

"I owe it to my wife, whose idea of a letter worked," he said. "Persistence paid off."

"When it's restored, I think it will be the lowest-mileage Superbird in the world."

The First '55 Vette

For at least four decades, Steve McCain has had a one-track mind for Corvettes. He decided early on that Chevrolet's fiberglass sports car was just his style, and he bought his first one—a 1965 model—while still in high school. While most of us would have been more than thrilled to impress our friends in the school parking lot with a (then) late-model Vette, McCain discovered his true automotive love.

"Back then, everyone who owned a Corvette automatically got a subscription to *Corvette News*," McCain said. "In one of those issues, they did a search for the oldest 1953 Corvette in existence. I thought the car looked really neat and decided I wanted one."

McCain lives in Summerfield, North Carolina, and the fifty-five-year-old collector put the word out among his car friends in the nearby Greensboro area. He got a lead on a 1954 Corvette that was sitting behind a house, but the owner wouldn't sell.

"I was excited, but he wouldn't sell; he was saving it for his son," he said.

The 1953 and 1954 Corvettes were virtually identical cars. Both were powered by the Blue Flame six-cylinder engine and were equipped with a two-speed automatic transmission. And most were painted white. Both are rare; only three hundred 1953 models were manufactured and 3,640 1954 Corvettes were built. In 1955, despite the optional V-8, only seven hundred Corvettes were built, because they were hard to sell.

"When Ford introduced the Thunderbird in 1955, nobody wanted to buy a Corvette," McCain said. "They were actually getting ready to discontinue the Corvette model."

More than thirty years ago, McCain had unearthed another lead. "My friend Larry Melvin told me about a Corvette in Lexington, North Carolina."

He drove about an hour to see the car. It belonged to the brother of the owner of The Corvette Center, a specialty shop in

Lexington. The '55 was parked behind the owner's parents' home nearby.

"The car was in pretty sad shape," McCain said. "My friend Bill Hampton went with me to check its credentials.

"I was told that on 1955 Corvettes, the serial number was on the steering column, but it wasn't," McCain said. "The owner didn't know either, and just walked away.

"We finally found the VIN tag on the driver's side doorjamb. Imagine our surprise when we saw the numbers."

The VIN read VE55S001001, which translates thusly:

V: V-8 Engine.

E: Corvette Series.

55: Model year.

S: St. Louis plant, where the car was produced.

001: All 1953–1955 Corvettes had the 001 designation.

001: The first car off the production line.

Steve McCain followed up a lead on a 1955 Corvette, one of seven hundred built, which was near Lexington, North Carolina. The car was in pretty sad condition, but at the $500 asking price, he feels he got a pretty good deal. *Steve McCain*

"I had always heard that Smokey Yunick got the first five Corvettes off the assembly line, but I guess not," he said.

McCain paid $500 for the car in 1970 and feels he got a pretty good deal.

Two years later, McCain heard of another early Corvette that was available, another 1955, for $1,000.

"It was in a junkyard in Wilkesboro [North Carolina], and was also in pretty sad shape," he said. "It had a big headrest that was molded into the rear trunk, holes in the frame, and holes where a small windscreen had been mounted. But it was a thousand dollars, and I just thought it was a botched up car, and I didn't want another '55, so I didn't buy it."

To this day, McCain regrets this decision because eventually he found out the Corvette was built by Zora Arkus-Duntov, and he had used it extensively at GM's Arizona test track.

McCain was hardly left empty-handed, though; he still had car number 001. The restoration of the first 1955 Corvette took four

This wasn't just any 1955 Corvette, though. Closer inspection revealed the serial number plate, indicating that it was the first Corvette to roll off the assembly line in 1955. *Steve McCain*

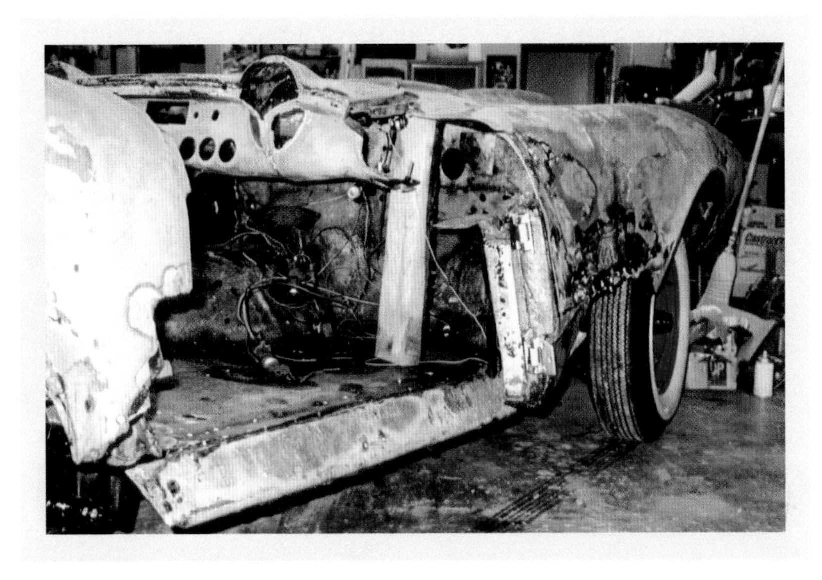

It took McCain four years to restore the Corvette. The early fiberglass work, rough even from the factory, had begun to deteriorate from sitting in the elements. *Steve McCain*

years. In 1976, he sold it for $10,000 to a collector who also had the first 1956 and the first 1957 Corvettes ever built.

Does he regret selling number 001? Sure, but McCain has owned many Vettes in his life, including one 1953, four 1954s, and the one 1955.

"If I still owned this car today, I think it would be more historically significant than the last 1967 big block, which got so much attention going into the [2007] Barrett-Jackson auction—and that was bid to more than six hundred thousand dollars," he said. "But these older cars just aren't as popular, so I'd say it would probably be worth two hundred thousand dollars."

An interesting side note, and a lesson on keeping in touch with people who own a car you'd like to acquire: Remember that first 1955 Corvette that McCain discovered behind a house in Lexington, but the guy was saving it for his son? Well in 1989, McCain received a call from the son who was looking to purchase his first home and wanted to sell the Corvette. He sold the car to McCain for $8,000.

After selling the first '55 Corvette, McCain built this former parts car into a hot rod, complete with widened body, LT-1 engine, and 700H transmission. Even used-up parts cars were recycled. *Steve McCain*

McCain used it as a parts car for a customized 1953 Vette he was restoring as a full custom (canted headlights, etc.).

That's not the end of the story yet. After the custom was completed, McCain turned his parts car into a hot rod. He widened the body and installed a late-model LT-1 drivetrain with a 700H automatic transmission. Then he painted it dark blue with scallops.

The moral? Corvettes are never scrapped—they are recycled!

The Pinto with a Pedigree

BY DON SHERMAN
TECHNICAL EDITOR OF *AUTOMOBILE* MAGAZINE

My barn find began with a surprise phone call from a stranger who told me he had a Pinto for sale.

The mention of Ford's star-crossed compact perked my ears. Long before flaming fuel tanks were hot news, I raced a red Ford Pinto in the budding SCCA Showroom Stock Sedan class. After it survived 25,000 miles in the hands of *Car and Driver* editors, Ford didn't want it back, so it became the magazine's first race car of the modern (post-1970) era.

That Pinto was my faithful steed at the 1972 SCCA driver's school I attended in Thompson, Connecticut (the same school that Paul Newman selected to start his illustrious motorsports career). The Pinto carried me to a second-place finish at my first race at Nelson Ledges (behind the indomitable F. Reed Andrews). In the fall of 1973, I led most of the first *Car and Driver* Challenge (editors versus readers) until I was unceremoniously crashed from contention by Bruce Cargill. Following a hasty repair in preparation for the Thanksgiving IMSA Radial Challenge race at Daytona, I crashed the same Pinto again on the drive to its transport trailer. My excuse was more legitimate this time; the competition brake pads we had installed were totally ineffective when traffic backed up on Manhattan's East River Drive, so I slammed into the back of some lady's Oldsmobile.

But forgive the detour—Bob Leier, the stranger, was not calling about *that* Pinto (may it rust in peace).

Enter Pinto II from the *Car and Driver* Hall of Racing Fame. This one followed my SS steed by one year. After the Lime Rock Reader's Challenge debacle (during which *Car and Driver* executive editor Patrick Bedard was also bunted from contention), we plotted our comeback. A Mazda RX-2 was constructed for campaigning

Car and Driver magazine editors didn't just write about racing; they raced, too! Showroom stock racing was their specialty, and they experimented with Mazdas, Vegas, Opels, and Pintos. Here the *Car and Driver* Pinto is competing in an IMSA Radial Sedan race in 1974 at Charlotte Motor Speedway, where it won.
Don Sherman Collection

IMSA's Radial Challenge series. Unfortunately, this rotary-powered racer was a bit too speedy for the officials' tastes; after only one season, a couple of pole positions, and two victories, it was banned from participation.

Pinto II was also comeback II. After studying the rulebook, Pat Bedard cagily concluded that an early Pinto powered by the new-for-1974 2.3-liter engine could give the reigning AMC Gremlins a run for the money, er, flag. As usual, he was correct. The score after five 1974 events was two poles, two wins at Charlotte, and three DNFs (a tire failure at Talladega and terminal engine problems at Lime Rock and Daytona).

While I was *Car and Driver's* technical editor during this period, my contribution to the IMSA Pinto effort was helping push the car from the pit after its engine blew at Daytona. While the Pinto was being groomed for the track, I was building a Mazda RX-3 for Bonneville. The very week I ran down the salt at 160 miles per hour to earn a record, Ron Nash and Pat Bedard co-drove the Pinto to one of its Charlotte victories.

When Stephan Wilkinson became *Car and Driver's* new editor in chief, he sent the Pinto packing.

"That would be my fault," Wilkinson acknowledged. "Under pressure from my boss, I chose to get *Car and Driver* out of the racing business and had the cars sold."

Enter Bob Leier.

Leier, who had previously raced Formula Fords in the Northeast, responded to *Car and Driver's AutoWeek* ad offering both the Pinto and the Mazda RX-2 to the highest bidders. The selling price for the Pinto and its trailer was about $4,500 (no one recalls the exact figure). Leier campaigned the car in one Canadian race and three IMSA races during the 1975 season, earning two respectable finishes.

Busy with his career and law school, Leier parked the Pinto. It spent one fall and winter stored outdoors, during which the interior

Thirty years after *Car and Driver* sold the Pinto, one of the magazine's former editors, Don Sherman, purchased the car back for $1,247. He trailered it to his Michigan garage and began restoration of the worn-out racer. *Don Sherman*

was invaded by leaves and vermin. Thereafter, it resided in the back corner of Leier's garage, first in Lexington, Massachusetts, later in Leesburg, Virginia. The engine was occasionally turned over, but not started. Leier harbored fond memories of his races with the Pinto and saved it hoping to revitalize it for vintage racing some day. Thirty years of decay later, a career change prompted a move to Florida and a burning desire to pass the Pinto on to someone who might carry out his dreams. I was that someone because Leier had discovered my car restoration hospital in Phil Berg's book, *Ultimate Garages*.

I first saw the Pinto upon raising the door on its Leesburg, Virginia, storage cell. The paint was dull and dusty; one tire was flat. Spare parts were stacked around and inside the car. Except for a cracked windshield and a front valence panel snagged out of shape by the last trip off the trailer, the corpse was in excellent shape with no apparent crash damage or rust. The glimmer of hope shining out of this dreary vault was that the Pinto was fully assembled with no major missing parts. Fellow journalist and amateur racer, Dan Carney, helped heave my prize onto its trailer for the trip home to Michigan.

For the most part, retrieving the Pinto from the barn was well orchestrated. In exchange for $1,247—a thousand for the car, the remainder to cover storage charges—Leier mailed the location and the lock-code information I needed. Chevrolet happened to be launching its new-for-2006 Tahoe SUV nearby, so I attended that meeting and requested use of the new vehicle for the trip home. An auto transport trailer was reserved at a nearby U-Haul dealer. Distance from the press launch location to the storage facility was only six miles, so every piece of the logistical puzzle dropped neatly into place. The only wild card was the weather; given the mid-December timing, snow was a distinct possibility.

Although snow was forecast, it held off until the last hundred or so miles of the five hundred-mile trip, and I rolled into my driveway without incident. Arrival photos, taken after a few hours

Sherman tore the car down to the bare shell and to his amazement found that it was in very good condition. He had to replace all of the fuel system components, but the engine and gearbox only needed inspection and cleaning. *Don Sherman*

of rest, look like a Christmas card with the Pinto blanketed by snow. My loving wife was not amused when I told her that a card attached to the car read, "To Cheryl, from Santa."

The hours spent on the Pennsylvania and Ohio turnpikes provided an excellent opportunity to formulate a game plan. I was happy to rescue what I considered a significant moment of automotive history from the shredder's jaws. My goal was to get the Pinto back into the pages of *Car and Driver* as a running, sparkling example of its former self. Following the revival process, it might enjoy a second life as a vintage racer. Eventually, the Pinto could retire in a museum or as part of a Ford fan's collection.

At least I wasn't bumbling along blindly. With three car and two motorcycle restoration projects under my belt, I was well aware that these revivals always exceed even the most ambitious estimates of the time and money required for completion. My goal was a running car by spring at any reasonable cost. Four months after the Pinto reached Michigan, its engine made the first ruckus in thirty years; two months after that, the Pinto moved out of the garage and down the street on its post-op shakedown drive.

The restoration process involved the usual strip-down, repaint, and reassembly. My intention was to preserve the car's integrity by incorporating only those changes necessary for it to return to the track as a vintage racer. Factoring in the thirty years of tuning and

Restored in just nine months, the Pinto hit the track for the first time since the mid-1970s for a shakedown test in 2006. The car ran and handled well and, to Sherman's surprise, didn't catch fire! *Morgan Segal*

technology enjoyed by its lucky peers (cars that survived to continue racing) was not part of the deal.

Of course, there were surprises. Leier's assurance that rust—the bane of every old car—would not be an issue was misguided. The lower hem flanges of both doors harbored major corrosion, so I replaced them with parts purchased from an Arizona salvage yard. To my amazement, I was informed that Pintos are indeed quite collectible and parts for them are currently in high demand. The engine and transmission passed inspection with such high marks that neither warranted a complete teardown. I removed and repaired a failed weld in the oil pan, but never separated the head from the block. I felt lucky to find most of the consumables, such as gaskets and chassis parts, still available from local parts outlets. The new windshield I needed was the last of its kind, and it was waiting patiently for me in a nearby warehouse.

That's not to say this job was a breeze. Except for the carburetor, everything touched by gasoline—the fuel cell, pumps, braided lines, etc.—had to be replaced. Since the electrical system lacked a single fuse or circuit breaker, I replaced both the wiring harness and the switch panel. An exhaust collector and dump pipe had to be fabricated. I also ditched the mechanically driven tachometer, updated the breaker points to electronic ignition, and replaced the out-of-date extinguisher bottle and restraint harness. The battery was relocated from the engine compartment to the trunk because contemporary rules allow that performance-enhancing alteration.

Aside from minor crash damage in the rear fender lips, the core structure including the roll cage and suspension modifications originally engineered by Patrick Bedard and fabricated by Ron Nash were perfectly sound. After sending the bare body shell out for media blasting, I hauled it to my trusty painter, John Monks. He sprayed three colors—light gray inside and underneath with white and blue for the exterior—in two steps with an in-between break to bolt in all the powertrain, chassis, hardware, plumbing, and electrical systems. I blame the painting process for this project taking twice as long as I initially planned.

My Pinto was officially finished in the fall of 2006, nine months after it rolled into Michigan. The first track test revealed the fun and speed I'd missed thirty years ago. To celebrate its revival, *Car and Driver* planned a gala reunion picnic with the Pinto, the RX-2, and a few veteran racer-writers in attendance.

Postscript

Gathering two veteran *Car and Driver* racers, two crotchety writers who drove them thirty years ago (Patrick Bedard and this correspondent), a technical editor with a fresh outlook (Aaron Robinson), a crack photographer (Morgan Segal), and a photo assistant was only slightly less complicated than the Normandy invasion. It all came together on a beautiful fall day at Firebird Raceway a few miles south of Phoenix. Miles of towing required: 4,350. Track rental cost: $2,500. Airline tickets purchased: 2. Miles driven by attendees: 1,200. Fun behind the two steering wheels: priceless.

Pat Bedard brought a scrumptious picnic lunch, but remained true to his retirement vows (from racing, not writing) by declining repeated urges to hot lap the machinery. Robinson and I had a great time flinging the old racers around Firebird's 1.1-mile short course, which consisted of a drag strip linked to a winding return road.

A reunion was held for the Pinto and another restored *Car and Driver* racer, a Mazda RX-2. Original drivers Pat Bedard (left) and Don Sherman brought the two racers to Firebird Raceway near Phoenix where the Pinto actually edged the Mazda in lap times and handling. *Morgan Segal*

Only one lunch-hour repair was necessary. To alleviate an interference condition between the driveshaft and its tunnel in bumpy turns, two spacers were removed from the Pinto's rear suspension. Problem solved.

After zillions of static, dynamic, and other digital photos were collected, I broke out my compact test equipment to gather a few performance stats. The RX-2's screaming rotary engine produced enough power to give that car a nine-mile-per-hour advantage at the end of the straightaway. The Pinto's Yokohama radials and lower stance gave it the cornering edge with a limit of 1.0g versus the Mazda's 0.92g. Braking abilities were about even. When the dust had settled, the Pinto edged out the RX-2 by a mere 0.2 seconds on its best lap. Average speed around the short course was in the mid-sixties (miles per hour) for both cars. With a bit more tuning and preparation, the Pinto with a pedigree will embark on its new life as a vintage racer.

Rescuing a Red Farmer Rust Bucket

Japanese cars from the 1970s are known as rust buckets. The metal on these cars was thin and rust-proofing was nonexistent. When rust invades a Datsun, Toyota, or Honda from that era, it's usually beyond fixing.

Unless it's an old race car.

Houghton Smith found an old Datsun 510 on a junk pile on Neal Cowles' farm in Ramer, Alabama, and dragged it off with a tractor. To the average person—or even the average car enthusiast—the car was worthless. That didn't stop Smith from paying top dollar for basically a very rusted shell.

That's because the car had some pedigree.

"The first time I saw that car race was when we got a sanction to host an IMSA race at Montgomery Speedway back in 1970," said Smith, who himself began to race a 750cc Abarth Allemano Cabriolet in 1964.

"The 510 was built by a couple of local oval track experts—Bo Freeman and Mike Hodgson—for Red Farmer to drive in that race."

Red Farmer is a legend in southern stock car racing culture. He is the founding member of the Alabama Gang, along with racers Bobby Allison and Neil Bonnett. The three of them became famous in the region for winning anything they raced before stepping up to NASCAR's top divisions.

Freeman and Hodgson went to the local Datsun dealer, bought a brand new Datsun 510 in a color that is known among Datsun enthusiasts as "baby poop brown," and built it into a race car. They called Peter Brock at the BRE Racing shops in California and ordered all the best pieces.

"When they built the original 1800cc engine, they were on the phone with Brock for a week straight!" Smith said.

Farmer was scheduled to race the newly built Datsun in the upcoming IMSA mini-stock race. It was highly unusual for the stock car driver to race in a compact sedan, but he was a major spectator draw for the inaugural oval-track event.

"He put on a pretty good show," Smith said. "In fact, he ran away with the show to the extent that IMSA threatened to take away his license—but he didn't care because he was really only interested in driving big cars anyway.

"He drove it just the one race, and that was it."

Interestingly, before the race started, Smith was invited to take a couple of laps around the track in the Datsun.

After the Montgomery race, Freeman and Hodgson converted the Datsun to road racing specs, and Max Long drove the car at a sports car race at Talladega Superspeedway.

Bobby and Nancy Taylor then purchased the car and raced it regionally at Charlotte Motor Speedway, Road Atlanta, and elsewhere.

When the car's road racing career came to an end, it was converted back to a mini-stock car and ran on oval tracks before being dismantled, towed up to Neal Cowles' farm, and basically forgotten.

On its maiden voyage, stock car legend Red Farmer leads in the Datsun 510 in an IMSA Mini-Stock race at Montgomery (Alabama) Speedway. The car handily won the race and IMSA officials asked him not to come back. *Houghton Smith Collection*

After changing hands and competing as an SCCA B-Sedan, the Datsun was stripped and put out to pasture on Neal Cowles' farm in Ramer, Alabama. This was where Houghton Smith found the once-proud racer. *Houghton Smith*

Until Smith got the bug to go vintage racing.

"I started to look around for a car to vintage race, and a couple of friends told me that the old 510 that Red Farmer raced would be legal to run in SVRA," Smith said. "So I decided to research the car's history. Luckily Bobby Taylor still had the car's logbooks, which were required at the time by the sanctioning body."

"But when I went up to look at it, the car was just a rusted shell with shotgun holes in the driver's door, and the interior was piled with oil drums, leaves, and garbage. Oh, and Bobby still had the original magnesium racing wheels for it, but there was nothing else."

Smith borrowed a tractor and pulled the car off the junk pile and on to a waiting trailer.

It was brought to Bobby and Nancy Taylor's race shop, where they cleaned, sandblasted, and restored it.

"So when I bought it, I really bought a set of logbooks, because even the roll bars were rusty," Smith said. "You could have poked a screwdriver through the pipes."

Now that he has fully restored the 510, Smith regularly competes in vintage races with the former junkyard dog. *Houghton Smith*

When it was restored, Red Farmer himself wanted to drive the car during parade lap ceremonies for the Talladega stock car race, but Smith regretfully had to turn him down. Smith was running for a vintage racing championship and was afraid that if the car was damaged at Talladega, he'd be unable to compete the following weekend.

Another famous Datsun 510 race car, the BRE guest race car, also resides in Montgomery, Alabama. It was driven by Bobby Allison and Peter Greg on occasion in the SCCA 2.5 Litre Trans-Am Series. That car was also restored by Bobby and Nancy Taylor for Smith's friend, Dennis Morgan.

"When you drive a 510, you wrestle it," Smith said. "No matter how you drive it, you get out sweating. It's a good handling car, but you have to drive it."

A Checkered Past

Some of Steve Contarino's fondest childhood memories come from the times he was invited to accompany his father to work driving taxis in the Massachusetts town of Lawrence. He remembers one day in 1973 in particular.

"I was waiting with my father in the cab stand for the return of his car from the previous shift when a very different car pulled to the curb," Contarino said. "It was car number twenty-three, and it was massive, much bigger than any of the GM or Ford cars he had driven in the past."

Contarino had just laid his eyes on his first Checker automobile.

"I was amazed at the look of the car," he said. "It was so massive; I thought to myself that a snowplow could go on the front."

That day left an impression on the youngster that continues today, more than thirty years later. (Perhaps his fixation with that service vehicle helped inspire him to start a business installing lights and sirens on about 2,200 brand new police cars every year.) It was no surprise that when Contarino began to collect cars, he bought two Checkers: a 1978 and a 1981.

Checker enthusiast Steve Contarino discovered probably the rarest of the breed—a Giugiaro-designed, Ghia-built prototype. The car was all but forgotten in a Washington State backyard when he read about it in the Checker club online newsletter. *Steve Contarino*

"They are both Model A-12s, the civilian versions of the car," he said. "The Model A-11 was the taxi version and had rubber floor mats. Ash trays and AM radios were optional."

Contarino is a member of the Checker Car Club of America, and one day as he was scanning the online newsletter, www.checkertaxistand.com, a car in the classified section got his attention. The ad mentioned Ghia and De Tomaso, yet it was for a Checker. Contarino read on... "1968 Checker Centurion Prototype. Designed by Giugiaro, built in Italy by Ghia. $50,000."

He began an intense search for information regarding this car and how it came to be.

At one time, Italian body company Ghia had a strong relationship with Chrysler Corporation. Ghia built large luxury limousines, such as stretched Imperials, for very wealthy individuals in this country and abroad. When that contract came to an end in the mid-1960s, the company began searching around for another American company to partner with through its U.S. affiliate, Rowan Industries in New Jersey—which also built experimental electric cars. The Italian firm decided that the oft-overlooked Checker would receive a Ghia makeover, and the huge car was unveiled at the 1968 Paris Auto Show. *Road & Track* described the Centurion in its January 1969 issue: "Very unexpected from an Italian coachbuilder was Ghia's Checker limousine, a great slab of real 'Big Mutha' with excessively deep windows and heavy flanks."

If Ghia desired attention, the coachbuilder certainly received it—good and bad—from the world's automotive press. The Checker drew extra attention—but suffered some unflattering comparisons—by virtue of its placement at the same display as the redesigned De Tomaso Mangusta.

A *Car and Driver* article described the Checker as "sinister," and said it appeared to have been commissioned by the mafia. But all reviewers agreed that it was a great improvement over the Checker's standard models, which were already beginning to show their age in the 1960s.

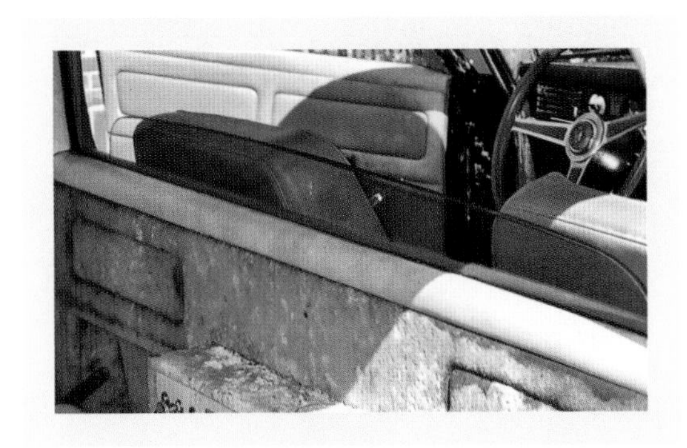

Mold and mildew took over the interior as the car sat in the moist environment for nearly thirty-five years. But for Contarino, who owns two other Checkers, the car will be restored to its former Paris show car condition.
Steve Contarino

After another show stop at the 1969 New York Auto Show, the Checker was mothballed. Ghia decided not to put the car into production, citing exorbitant retooling costs.

John Ellis, then president of Rowan Industries, decided the Ghia Checker would be just the ticket for use at his vacation home in Florida, and he used the car there for about one year before trading it for some Washington acreage in 1971. Unfortunately, Ellis was never able to enjoy his new real estate; he died in a plane crash that same year.

The collector world lost track of the car as it languished under a tarp in a Washington State backyard from 1971 until 2005.

The Ghia Checker resurfaced when a water meter reader asked about the car, which had been hidden from view of the road. Current owner Contarino estimates the meter reader purchased the car for $500. He then posted it on the Checker website.

"He was looking for fifty thousand dollars for it," said Contarino, who negotiated with the gentleman for a month or two. "I was at the Barrett-Jackson Auction trying to buy a Chrysler Airflow, but it sold for more than I had hoped. Then I got a call on my cell phone from this guy with the Checker."

"I talked him down from $50,000 to $20,000, then to $15,000, to $12,000, and we ended up making the deal at $10,000."

Contarino has since had a professional appraisal, and the Checker's value when restored should be in excess of $100,000.

An original press release photo. The Checker prototype was hyped in magazines such as *Road & Track*, but the car never really created the "buzz" that Checker had hoped. So the idea was scrapped, and the prototype was ultimately sold. *Steve Contarino Collection*

After the car arrived at his Massachusetts home, he removed the engine and brought the car to a shop for a body-off restoration. He figures he'll have about $60,000 invested in the Checker when it is completed.

Investigating his new purchase, Contarino discovered that a standard Checker frame was utilized. Additionally, the standard-issue Chevy 283-cubic-inch engine and Powerglide transmission were used. But the coachwork was definitely not standard.

"It's really odd, but the car has a rear suicide door on the driver's side, but the passenger side rear door is conventional," he said. "The Italian craftsmanship is unbelievable, the best in the world."

"The body held up real well after all those years under a tarp in Washington's humid climate. But the interior took the brunt of it; the leather and trim pieces have bad mildew damage and corrosion."

Perhaps Checker should have considered producing the Centurion, because by 1982—sixty years after producing its first car—the last Checker rolled off the Kalamazoo, Michigan, assembly line. Checker remains in business today as a metal stamping supplier for other car companies, but its days as an auto manufacturer are over.

Now that Contarino has fulfilled his dream of owning a Checker—the rarest in the world, no less—what's next?

"I like cars with mystery," he said. "Next I'd like to have a Tucker, which was surrounded with both mystery and controversy."

Perhaps one still exists in a backyard somewhere.

Smokey and the Boss

In the 1960s and 1970s, the SCCA Trans-Am Series had a special sex appeal to car racing fans. Legendary drivers did battle in one of history's most competitive race series, and the cars were the most popular muscle cars ever built.

Late 1960s and early 1970s Camaros, 'Cudas, Challengers, Javelins, and Mustangs were heavily modified by major teams like Penske or Bud Moore and duked it out on road circuits like Laguna Seca, Lime Rock, and Bridgehampton. Those brutal machines are now some of the hottest commodities in the high-priced muscle car collector market.

Friends Ross Myers and Terry Bookheimer have developed a talent for seeking out and purchasing the Ford products that competed in the early SCCA Trans-Am Series. They started buying these cars in the early 1980s, before they became popular, and have since developed quite an impressive vintage racing team. These cars have been restored and race regularly at vintage events throughout the United States.

1970 Boss 302 Mustang

"This was the first car we bought," Bookheimer said. "We both attended Trans-Am races in 1970 and 1971. Ross was into antique cars, but after I told him about the open track days at the Shelby convention, I said, 'Ross, you've got to try this.' So I started to look around for an old race car, even though I didn't know anything about them."

Bookheimer saw a small ad in *Hemmings Motor News* that read: Factory-backed Trans-Am Mustang, One-of-a-kind, Syracuse, New York. He called the phone number and was connected to a bar. Bookheimer thought the bar owner might own the car, but instead, the seller lived above the tavern.

"I'll have him call you back," said the barkeep.

"The guy was a derelict," Bookheimer said. "Finally when he called me back, it was a collect call."

Privateer Ed Hinchliff drove this Boss 302 as an independent in the glory days of the Trans-am racing in 1970. It's the car that led Ross Myers and Terry Bookheimer into Trans-Am race car collecting. Here it's racing in a non–Trans-Am event at Watkins Glen. *Myers/Bookheimer Collection*

"I negotiated with the guy for six months. Obviously the market still hadn't caught up with these cars. I drove up to look at it. It had an SCCA brass tag applied to the roll bar, but no VIN number."

"'How come there is no serial number?' I asked the seller. 'I don't know,' he said."

Bookheimer soon realized that the reason the seller knew so little about the race car was because he didn't actually own it. He was apparently selling it on spec for the actual owner.

The Mustang was originally built by Ford engineer Ed Hinchliff, whose father was a vice president at Ford. His father was able to secure a bare body-in-white 1970 Mustang for his son to build into a race car. The younger Hinchliff spent all of 1970 building the car into a Trans-Am racer, with help from Ford's factory Trans-Am supplier, Kar Kraft.

"Whenever Kar Kraft lunched a motor on the dyno, they'd call Ed and tell him to come and pick it up out of the dumpster,"

This is how Bookheimer discovered the car at a body shop storage yard in New York in June 1983. The car had been stripped of most of its racing goodies, but for a thousand dollars, he feels he got the best of the deal. *Bookheimer*

Bookheimer said. "He got all the good parts basically for free."

Hinchliff raced the car in the last two 1970 Trans-Am races, and the entire 1971 season.

"He had three top-ten finishes, including a seventh and an eighth, which was quite respectable for a private guy without sponsorship," Bookheimer said.

After the 1971 season, Hinchliff sold the car to Roger Pierce of Syracuse, New York. Pierce raced the car in local SCCA races, but during that time, the car was hit hard in a racing accident. Pierce cosmetically repaired the car and ran it in another couple of races before parking it for good behind a body shop.

"He stripped it for parts and basically junked it," Bookheimer said. "It sat in the storage yard behind the body shop from 1974 until 1981. I was hesitant to buy the car until Pierce told me it was originally Hinchliff's, but after I spoke to him, I decided to buy it."

It was a lucky day for Bookheimer, because not only did he get an authentic Trans-Am Mustang, but Hinchliff still had lots of spare parts for the car—wheels, tires, transmissions, and suspension pieces. And it was all purchased for $1,000.

The car has since been entered in many vintage races, beginning at the 1986 SVRA races at Mid Ohio.

Now that they've restored it, Myers and Bookheimer regularly compete in vintage Trans-Am events with the car. *Myers/Bookheimer Collection*

Smokey's Trans-Am Car

Mechanical wizard Smokey Yunick was well known as a builder of NASCAR stockers and even the occasional Indy car, but most people are not aware Smokey once owned a Trans-Am car. That prize now resides in Myers' and Bookheimer's garage.

The Kar Kraft company of Dearborn, Michigan, built seven Trans-Am Mustangs in 1969; three went to Bud Moore, three went to Carroll Shelby, and one went to Smokey Yunick. Yunick's was built under orders of new Ford President Bunkie Knudsen, who had developed a friendship with Yunick when he ran Pontiac.

"Paint one up for Smokey," said Knudsen, who had Kar Kraft paint one black and gold, the colors Yunick had made famous in Daytona and Indianapolis. It was the only completed car of the seven turned out by Kar Kraft; the rest were sent to Moore and Shelby in only partially completed form. Yunick's car had a completed suspension, was fully wired, and had a race-modified Boss

302 engine, all ready for track action—but Yunick never used the car for Trans-Am racing.

After the car was delivered to Yunick's Daytona Beach shop, he pulled the 302 engine and replaced it with a 427. He and his crew also removed the disc brakes and fitted drums. Yunick was turning the Mustang into a NASCAR Baby Grand stocker for driver Buddy Baker to enter at Talladega.

Baker dominated the first three-quarters of the race until the 427 broke a rocker arm and ended his day. The car never ran in a Trans-Am race.

Yunick sold the car to a Texan, who ran the Mustang as a Modified racer. As such, the doors were hollowed out and welded shut, and a NASCAR roll cage was fitted.

The once-beautiful black-and-gold Boss 302 was used up and put away wet, the fate of many short-track racers. Eventually, it was sold to a man in Houston who collected Boss 302s. It sat in his shed for a number of years.

"Once we got into these Trans-Am cars, we heard about the car's existence through the grapevine," Bookheimer said. "We got a call in 1987 or 1988 from a guy who said that he knew where the seventh Kar Kraft 302 was buried, the old Smokey Yunick car."

"What Smokey Yunick car? Most people didn't even know about the car because it was only driven once and put away. It was forgotten," he added.

Bookheimer went down to Houston to meet the owner, who was a drag racer. He had a drag racing Boss 302 and a concours restored Boss 302, but didn't have much appreciation for the old racer sitting in his shed. The owner had purchased it cheap in the early 1980s with no intention of restoring it. Bookheimer checked the numbers and the brass Kar Kraft tag that was attached to the roll cage. He negotiated with the man and paid an outrageous price at the time—$20,000.

The car was hauled back to Pennsylvania nonstop on a trailer in thirty-four hours, with Bookheimer and his brother-in-law trading off between sleeping and stints and the wheel.

Sitting in front of Kar Kraft headquarters in 1969, the just-completed Boss 302 was soon shipped to legendary race car builder Smokey Yunick in Daytona Beach, Florida. *Myers/Bookheimer Collection*

"Thankfully, the car still had many of its original Trans-Am parts: the original Monroe shocks, the trick front A-arms, and the full-floater rear end," he said.

Bookheimer explains that proper Trans-Am cars are easy to identify because they were ordered as Sport Roof Mustangs with 351-cubic-inch engines (which were then swapped for 302s) and no sound-deadening materials. And all the cars had production VIN numbers.

Myers and Bookheimer turned the car over to a top-notch restoration shop in Ohio, the same team that restored Myers' Peter Revson Boss 302 and one of the Penske Javelins. The car was completed in time for the 1995 Monterey Historic races and has been raced regularly since.

"In 1969, these cars ran with dual quads, so the throttle is like an on-off switch," Bookheimer said. "It's a handful."

After years of hard racing in the NASCAR circuit, this is how the former Smokey Yunick Boss 302 was discovered in a Texas storage building in the late 1980s. *Myers/Bookheimer Collection*

Now restored, this is the ex–Dick Thompson notchback Mustang that won the first pole at the first Trans-Am race at Sebring in 1966. The car, which was for sale as a basketcase in Alabama, was sitting next to a certain Cougar that Myers was interested in. *R. Harrington*

Driven hard and put away wet might best describe the condition of this former Dan Gurney Trans-Am Cougar in 1969. Myers and Bookheimer purchased it in a package deal along with the Dick Thompson Mustang. *Myers/Bookheimer Collection*

Trans-Am Double Dip

Myers and Bookheimer were on a roll. The team was amassing a nice collection of Trans-Am cars, racing them, and having fun. They started to follow up other leads for significant cars. One day Myers got a call that a special car might available in Alabama.

"I went down to look at a Mustang notchback race car," Myers said. "It had been raced by Washington, D.C., dentist Dick Thompson, who won the first pole position in Trans-Am at the Sebring race in 1966."

When Myers walked into the storage building where the Mustang coupe was being stored, another car caught his attention.

"I saw this tired, old blue race car," he said. "It was a Mercury Cougar. I tried not to act excited."

Myers casually asked about the Cougar.

"Hey, what about that car?" he asked. "'Oh, that's just an old race car, you wouldn't be very interested in it,' the guy told me."

Restored, the 1967 Cougar has become the gem in the Myers/Bookheimer Trans-Am collection. The car retains it Hi-Po 289 engine with two four-barrel carburetors. It even has the stock Cougar steering wheel, just like when Gurney raced it. *Bob Dunsmore*

Still showing his interest in the Thompson Mustang, he asked again about the Cougar.

"It's the '67 Cougar that Dan Gurney raced in the Trans-Am," the seller said. "Afterwards, it was raced by Tiny Lund in the Baby Grand division."

But the seller said he wasn't very interested in selling the Cougar.

Myers and the seller walked around looking at the other cars in this man's collection and finally came back to the notchback. It was negotiation time.

"The notchback was a terrific car," Myers said. "But as I was looking at that Mustang, I was thinking about the Cougar. Finally, it came to a point when I had to make a decision."

Myers, a successful businessman, plied his best sales skills.

"I told him I'd make him a package deal for the pair of cars, the Mustang and the Cougar," Myers said. "He really didn't want to sell the Cougar, but we finally closed the deal.

"As it turns out, the two cars I bought that day are my favorite race cars to drive."

High-Tech Barn Finder

Pay attention, because Mark Gold is going to let you in on a little trade secret. He has developed a new method for searching for old cars, and it doesn't involve donning old boots and venturing out into the countryside to traipse through muddy fields and peer into cow barns. In fact, Gold has found and purchased some of the most desirable cars on the planet without leaving his desk. Or his keyboard.

Using his method, Gold has so far discovered and purchased an experimental Cobra and a Shelby GT500, and he's just started to pursue a Ferrari Daytona. And through the kindness of his heart, he has decided to share his approach with our readers.

Ever the entrepreneur, Gold owns a speeding ticket agency based in Miami. His business—The Ticket Clinic (www.theticketclinic.com)—represents drivers with speeding citations from all over the United States.

In order to remain competitive in his industry, Gold has become savvy in the ways of internet commerce and web-based marketing. So being the car collector that he is, he naturally has used the internet—mostly eBay—to look for his dream cars . . . in Europe.

You see, to search for a car on eBay in the United States, you would simply type www.ebaymotors.com into your computer's search engine. The "com" designates United States commerce. Conversely, if someone in England were to search for a car on eBay, he would most likely type in www.ebaymotors.uk; the "uk" designation signifying United Kingdom, or England. So someone in the United States searching for, say, a Jaguar, would never be aware of all the potential Jaguars available in England if he only typed in the "com" designation.

"I've found that a lot of people who sell cars aren't very Internet savvy," said the fifty-one-year-old Gold, a native of Long Island. "A lot of guys in Europe don't advertise on U.S. websites."

"So I just started checking out eBay car listings using other country designations: IT for Italy, DE for Germany, etc."

And Gold's method has produced, well, gold.

Realizing that sports car buyers in the future would want more creature comforts (roll-up windows, folding top, etc.), product planners at AC began sketching the next-generation Cobra, shown here in a factory rendering. *Mark Gold Collection*

THE SPANISH-AMERICAN SHELBY

Gold has always loved the products of legendary race driver Carroll Shelby, so he searched on eBay's England site for a GT500, and was surprised at what he found.

Back in 1967, Ford Motor Company shipped a 1967 Shelby GT500 to exhibit at the Fair of Seville in Italy. After the fair, the Shelby remained in Europe, years later winding up in Madrid, Spain, with 32,000 miles on the odometer and its engine removed. A Mustang restorer in England purchased the car from its Spanish owner for 300,000 pesetas, and brought it home to England. The car was hastily restored, but soon thereafter purchased by a renowned Mustang restorer, who redid the work properly. Upon completion, the lime gold four-speed car was featured in many English car magazines and rated the best Shelby in Europe.

When that owner put the car up for sale, he listed it only on eBaymotors.uk, therefore ignoring the world's largest Shelby market, the United States.

"Nobody in the United States even knew about this car," Gold said. "I was bidding in British pounds sterling, and wound up purchasing the car for the equivalent of eighty-thousand pounds, about one hundred forty thousand dollars U.S. This was in October 2005, when similarly prepared Shelbys were selling at auctions for between two hundred forty-five thousand and four hundred seventy-one thousand dollars."

"And nobody even bid against me," said Gold.

Thrilled with his success, Gold decided to go one step further and pursue the car of his childhood dreams, a 289 Cobra.

The Devonshire Prototype

In the early 1960s, the AC sports car was beginning to show its age. Its roots went back to the early 1950s with the Tojeiro Bristol, with its primitive leaf-spring suspension and nearly complete lack of creature comforts. So, doing what the head of any large company should do, Derek Hurlock, chairman of AC Cars, began developing the next generation sports car to replace the AC Ace, AC Bristol, and ultimately the Cobra.

The prototype, one-of-one and serial number MA 200, was a new design from the chassis up. The developers named it Cobra after the most competitive of the AC-derived cars. The new chassis utilized a F1-type pivoting steering system superior to AC's early worm-and-sector and later the rack-and-pinion designs. The new space frame had its front shocks mounted inboard, and was equipped with a five-speed ZF gearbox backing up a 271-horsepower high-performance 289 Ford engine.

Its styling, though, was the most radical change over the prior Cobra's Ace-based lines. The rear more closely resembles an Alfa Romeo or Ferrari of the period; up front is a more aerodynamic shape, presaging the look of an Italia, which was to follow a couple of years later.

Only the one car was built, referred to internally as the AC V-8 Exp (Experimental). Because of financial issues or weak consumer interest, the design was ultimately scuttled. But not before the December 1964 issue of *Road & Track* announced in Miscellaneous

Ramblings that "a prototype AC Cobra has been seen on the roads of England, giving cause to many rumors."

The prototype changed hands several times over the following decades, until our eBay hunter Mark Gold began to pursue it.

"I was playing around on Google.co.uk, looking for a 289 Cobra, and this pops up," Gold said. "It looks like a cross between an Aston Martin and a Jensen Healey. So I called the owner and he tells me the story of MA 200.

"I fell in love with the car because it's real and significantly less expensive than a 289 Cobra. I sent a deposit off to Devonshire, England, and asked for additional paperwork."

Gold quickly closed the deal. Once he took possession of the car, he began to realize just how different this car was from a traditional 289 Cobra. For instance, it's about eight inches longer, and at 2,650-pounds, it is much more of a Grand Tourer in character. It is right-hand drive, and even though it was originally equipped with wire wheels, it is now equipped with Minilites.

Since taking delivery of the car, Gold has communicated with a number of engineers and mechanics who were involved in its design and construction.

With new AC Cobras visible in the showroom window, AC's only prototype of the new design is put on the road for evaluation. Because of financial issues, the car was never developed and fell into private ownership. *Mark Gold Collection*

"I have photographs of the car under construction at the factory with the Ford V-8 sitting in it," Gold said. "And I just paid one hundred dollars for the original one-to-one drawings of the car's profile and suspension."

So what does Gold have here? It's hard to say. He loves the car, and said it fulfills his lifelong desire to own a Cobra. But what about the value? Is it worth more than a 289 Cobra because of its rarity, or is it simply a curiosity with a questionable valuation? With one-offs it's always hard to guess because there are no other examples for comparison.

Gold doesn't seem to care. He loves the car. And he points out that he didn't buy this car twenty years ago, or even ten years ago. He purchased it in July 2006.

Such cars are still out there.

"I spend two to four hours a day scanning the internet for car deals, which might not be healthy," he said. "My wife has recently given me a book on how to overcome your obsessions!"

Gold is now scanning the web for a Ferrari Daytona.

Looking more like a Daimler 250 SP or a Lotus Elan, Mark Gold's AC prototype sits in his driveway in Florida. He continues to search for cars around the world via the internet, especially on eBay. *Mark Gold*

Looking similar to an AC Cobra under the hood, Gold's Hi-Po 289-powered prototype was built as an engineering and marketing study. It was a major departure from AC's sports car product line. *Mark Gold*

"There are currently twenty-nine Daytonas for sale in Europe," he said. "Guys just looking for a Daytona in the United States won't see half that many. The biggest obstacle is dealing with the various languages across Europe. But you'd be surprised; nearly everyone speaks at least a little English."

"I'll narrow it down to five cars, and then hire someone to take a look at them. I've bought six cars on eBay, and I've never been burned. The cars have generally been better than I expected."

That's not to say there are no duds or bum deals to be had on the internet. But the point is that this is a research tool—perhaps the best way ever to hunt down cars worldwide. Then it's up to you to ensure the car is sound before you actually part with cash.

Leno's Duesies

Duesenbergs are very, very rare. For example, Ford built fifteen million Ford Model Ts while Duesenberg built a total of 481 Model J, SJ, and JN cars during the Depression era of 1928 to 1937.

Duesenbergs were also very expensive.

When a new Ford Model A roadster could be had for $380, Duesies sold for between $16,000 and $25,000, even more for a few cars with custom coachwork.

"People who bought these cars new were Fortune 500–type guys," said Randy Ema of Orange, California. Ema is a Duesenberg expert. He's also the guy Duesenberg enthusiast Jay Leno relies on for advice on his favorite brand of car.

When Duesenbergs were built, they were without question the finest cars in the world, surpassing Rolls-Royce, Mercedes, and Hispano-Suiza in power, ride, and technical sophistication. In the 1930s, an unsupercharged Model J produced a claimed 265 horsepower from its twin-cam, thirty-two-valve straight-eight engine—quite a lot when Ford V-8s of the same era, considered powerhouses, produced just 85 horsepower.

The most advanced cars built at the time, Duesenbergs were packed with innovative features, including a self-lubrication feature on the Model J. Owners included kings, princes, gangsters, religious leaders, and celebrities such as William Randolph Hearst, Howard Hughes, Gary Cooper, and Clark Gable.

And now Jay Leno.

In addition to nearly a hundred other interesting cars, Leno owns several Duesenbergs, and he is somewhat of an authority on the marque. So when he heard about a couple of "forgotten" Duesenbergs, he was all ears.

1927 Duesenberg Model X

"When people see me on TV and learn that I'm a car collector, they want me to see their cars," said the host of NBC's *Tonight Show*.

"Sometimes they want me to own their cars."

Such was the case with the 1927 Duesenberg Model X garaged in Burbank, California, just a few miles from the NBC Studios where Leno works each day.

"This guy named Harry owned a garage and was a race car enthusiast," Leno said. "He bought this old Duesenberg for three hundred dollars out of Chicago back in 1946, probably with the intention of restoring it."

Harry had the car transported to California on a train. Because his purchase had a blown engine, Harry tied a chain around his car's bumper and towed the Duesenberg from the station to his house in Burbank.

He put it in his garage behind the house, locked the door, and didn't open it again for almost sixty years.

"I always knew Harry had something interesting in his garage," Leno said. "He had a Duesenberg racing engine that had

Comedian Jay Leno didn't have to go far to uncover a real Duesie barn find. This 1927 Duesenberg Model X had been hidden in a Burbank, California, garage just a few miles from the NBC Studios from 1946 until it was unearthed in 2004. *Randy Ema*

won at Indianapolis stored in a box in his yard. But he'd never let me inside the garage.

"I'd drive by his house with my Stanley Steamer, blow the horn—beep-beep—and take him for a ride around town. But still he kept the contents of the garage a secret.

"'Hey, Harry, what's in the garage?' I'd say. 'Wouldn't you like to know,' is all he'd answer."

But when Harry was ninety-two years old, and about to enter a nursing home, he called Leno and said he could go into the garage—which was no easy task, since earthquakes over the years had made the doors almost impossible to open.

When Leno and his friend Ema finally got inside, it was like he was walking into a time capsule.

"There were newspapers stacked up in there with news about the end of World War II," Leno said. "There were Orange Crush soda cans and old porcelain signs from the era."

It's amazing what a little soap and water can do! Leno decided not to restore the Model X, but instead just cleaned it up. Here it is on the lawn at Pebble Beach in 2005. *Randy Ema*

According to Ema, thirteen Model Xs were built, and four exist today.

"It was nice enough, but had a worn-out engine," Ema said. "Thank goodness Harry left the windows closed, so there were no moths or mice in the interior."

Harry had had a change of heart, and now he wanted Leno to own the car. Leno negotiated with Harry's daughter, who, although she lived in the house nearly all her life, knew nothing of the prestigious car in the backyard garage. Leno wanted the car, but wanted to be fair about the price, so he suggested that the family have appraisers come in and determine a price. Leno agreed with their price, and he made the purchase, not only of the Model X, but the entire contents of the garage.

"I bought all sorts of neat items—the signs, old parts," he said. "There was also another Duesenberg in the garage, a Model A that had been hacked up with some kind of Packard body."

The Model X car was in good enough condition when it was pulled from the garage that Leno made the decision to not restore the car. "I'm going to keep it just the way it is," he said.

The car has already been displayed on the lawn at the Pebble Beach Concours and was featured in a Discovery Channel special.

1931 Duesenberg Model J

Leno had heard the rumors about a Model J Duesenberg—the most prestigious model in the company's line—for at least ten years. The stories revolved around a tale that in the early 1930s, the original owner of a Duesenberg parked it in a garage in New York City and never came back to pick it up. But according to Leno, stories of Duesenbergs are many, and almost none are true.

"There are some vehicles—Vincent Motorcycles, Alfa Romeos, some Harley-Davidsons—that have myths that develop around them," Leno said. "Duesies are certainly that type of vehicle."

Leno was not able to resist the appeal of the myth. While he and his wife were in New York City for a shopping trip several years ago, he decided to take a side trip and do a little hunting.

"I'm not much of a shopper, so I decided to hit public garages and see if I could actually find some of these lost New York City collector cars that I'd always heard about," he said. "I'd go up to a garage operator and ask if there were any old cars in there, and they'd say 'Sure.' And sometimes you'd find a 1920s Rolls-Royce, and sometimes you'd find a Ford Maverick."

"Eventually I walked into a garage on West 57th Street off Park Avenue, and the guy said to go upstairs and take a look. There, on the third floor, next to the window, was the Duesenberg I'd heard about."

The myth was true.

"It was the last unrestored, original owner Duesenberg on Earth," Ema said. "It was a 1931, was parked in the garage in 1933, and not removed for seventy years. It only had 7,085 miles on the odometer. The original upholstery would have been in great shape, but someone piled a bunch of old tires in the car about fifty years ago, so the chemicals in the rubber stained and ruined the interior."

The car had a Woods Body mounted to the Duesenberg chassis. Woods, according to Leno, was the body company that built President Abraham Lincoln's funeral coach.

The car was parked next to a window that was always open. According to Ema, there was six inches of dirt all around the car because nobody had swept around it in almost three-quarters of a century.

And because there was a small leak above the car, when it rained, over seventy years—drip, drip, drip—a hole developed in the fender.

"Other people had known about this car," Leno said. "I had heard about the hidden New York Duesenberg for years, but when I actually found it, I didn't want to lose it. So I made up a story—no, it was an absolute lie—that the car couldn't be removed from its third-floor home because the new elevator that had been installed several years earlier was too small to fit the car."

Leno contacted the Duesie's owner, and he heard those words so many of us barn finders hate to hear: "No, it's not for sale."

This 1931 Model J Duesenberg (on the left) sat for seventy years in a New York City parking garage before being found and purchased by Leno. The car's interior and exterior had deteriorated because it sat next to an open window for so long. *Randy Ema*

But then he heard from a friend that it might, in fact, be for sale, but the matter was complicated.

Since the car had sat for so long, and the original owner's son was behind on paying for the storage, there was about $80,000 owed in parking fees. So when most of the people who had known about the car offered $10,000, the owner simply said no.

"The highest offers he received were about $35,000 to $45,000, but it was worth more than $100,000," said Leno. "So when I offered the owner fair market value, he jumped at it. I think I got it for a good price, and I didn't treat these people like idiots."

The Duesenberg was trucked from New York to California, where it was delivered first to Ema's shop, where it was inventoried and cleaned up. Then it was delivered to Leno's Big Dog Garage.

According to Leno, this car will be sympathetically restored.

"It's just a little too far gone to be preserved," he said.

Leno isn't finished with searching for forgotten cars. He's on the hunt for a couple of intriguing cars he recently heard about.

Once the Model J was removed from its "Manhattan tomb" and inspected, Leno decided the car needed to be restored from the ground up. He is now in the middle of that restoration in the Burbank facility known as Big Dog Garage. *Randy Ema*

"There's a 1933 Cadillac that was apparently put on blocks and properly stored in 1935," he said. "It's still owned by the woman who bought it new. She's ninety-five years old."

And he has learned that the same gentleman who bought the Duesenberg Model J also bought a Bugatti in 1936 or 1937. And it, too, is hidden somewhere in New York City. But Jay's not speaking.

"I think lots of old stuff that was found in the 1960s is going to come back on the market," he said.

And Leno is going to try to own as many of those old relics as he can.

CHAPTER FOUR

Stranger Than Fiction

The Mob GTO

Lake Placid, New York, is a small town tucked away in the Adirondack Mountains about one hundred miles south of the Canadian border. It's the type of area where people know each other's business, and secrets are rare.

Twenty years ago, Rob Bugbee chose this community as his new home, chucking the pressures of his ABC Sports job to pursue his passion for old cars. Bugbee opened Alpine Restorations, which specializes in making neglected muscle cars look new.

You'd imagine that as the owner of an automotive restoration business in this tiny community, Bugbee would know about every car for miles around. Not necessarily.

Rob Bugbee followed up on a lead about an old GTO in a garage near his Lake Placid, New York, home. After he purchased and inspected it, he discovered that the highly optioned convertible, formerly owned by a mobster, was perhaps the rarest GTO in existence. *Rob Bugbee*

As my friend Bill Warner knows all too well, sometimes terrific cars can be discovered—or not discovered—just blocks away from your own home. And all car collectors can tell stories of losing a terrific car that was right under their nose.

Bugbee is the third owner of a 1968 Pontiac GTO convertible that had been sitting about one mile from his house in Wilmington, New York, for more than thirty years. He later found he was one of the few people who didn't know about the car.

"A friend of mine called and said he was moving, and he had to get rid of this old muscle car in his garage," Bugbee said. "He rented a garage storage spot to this guy about thirty years earlier, but the guy never paid any rent and never picked it up, so finally he just had to find a new home for it.

"So I went down there, and the car was surrounded with old bicycles and other junk."

Thankfully, the car was covered and was sitting on jack stands.

"I said to myself, 'Wow, it's a convertible and it's got a four speed,'" he said.

But Bugbee didn't want to pay the amount being asked for the car, so he waited about six weeks before he wheeled and dealed with his friend for the best price.

Bugbee won't say how much he paid for the car in 2003, but said it was less than the $5,037.14 list price that the car sold for when new.

"It was dirt cheap," he said. "I didn't realize what it was. I thought I'd just fix it up and flip it for a profit."

But when Bugbee got the car back to his shop and began cleaning it up, he became interested in some of the markings and codes under the hood.

"I'm looking at the production codes, and it said Ram Air II, so I called a friend of mine in Michigan who really knows Pontiacs," he said. "I gave him all the codes, and he wasn't very familiar with them, so he told me he'd call me back."

"When he called, he said, 'I hope you're sitting down, because you just bought the rarest GTO on Earth!' I'm looking at the phone and saying, 'You've got to be kidding me.'"

Bugbee said that this car had been casually for sale for about twenty years.

"Every car guy in the area had heard about it, and I was the last one to hear about it," he said. "But since the rumors were that the car had a blown engine and a blown rear, nobody was interested."

The car, VIN number 242678B130848, had been ordered in 1968 with twenty-five options, which was very unusual—and expensive—in those days. The original Long Island owner is rumored to have been connected with the mob. But this mobster had good taste in cars. He ordered the black-on-black with gold interior convertible from Triangle Pontiac in Queens with virtually every option available.

The GTO's Protect-O-Plate specifications list shows that the car is equipped with engine code XS, which designates a 400-cubic-inch,

360-horsepower Ram Air engine. When ordered with the manual transmission, the compression ratio was an aggressive 10.75:1. Bugbee said that power output is above the engine's 366 rated horsepower.

"It's probably closer to four hundred twenty-five horsepower if you do the math," he said. "Basically, the car was built with a detuned racing engine. These cars aren't very pleasant to drive around town; they don't make good grocery getters."

Bugbee discovered that the car's 4.33 rear-end ratio had been damaged sometime in its life. Since a timing slip from New York National Speedway was discovered in the glove box, a blown rear didn't surprise him. But the good news is that Bugbee located a correct ZL-code 4.33 rear that had been sitting on a collector's shelf for eighteen years.

Some of the other options on the car include a hood-mounted tach, power disc brakes, Rally II Wheels, a handling package, AM/FM radio, power windows, power antenna, remote trunk release, wood steering wheel and shift knob, lighted ignition switch, under-hood lamp, trunk lamp, console, vanity mirror, door edge guards, hidden headlights, cornering lamps, exhaust tips, and spare tire cover.

"No dealer would have ordered that many options," Bugbee said. "They all add up to sixteen hundred dollars, which was a huge amount for 1968."

At some point, the original owner must have tired of owning his car, so he passed it to the second owner, who purchased it with 48,000 miles on the clock. Owner number two put it into longtime storage with about 52,000 miles on it, which is what the odometer still reads.

Bugbee brought the car back to his shop and quickly got it running, even with thirty-year-old fuel in the tank. He discovered that the car was in amazing condition without a speck of rust.

Even though Bugbee is a dyed-in-the-wool Chevy guy, he quickly learned all he could about Pontiacs.

The 1968 Ram Air II car was equipped with twenty-five factory options, including this rare hood-mounted tachometer. *Rob Bugbee*

"There is only one other four-speed convertible like mine, but it has only three or four options," he said. "And there is an automatic convertible that is known as well. There were six or eight convertibles originally built with the Ram Air II engine and about two hundred forty-three hardtops."

"Everyone has been looking for Judge convertibles, but for real Pontiac collectors, my car is the one missing from all the big collections."

Since purchasing the GTO, Bugbee has simply cleaned up the car, and he has no plans to restore it. In 2003, he trailered the car to Pontiac, Michigan, for the twenty-fifth GTO Association of America National Convention. He brought it there simply to show fellow enthusiasts what he had found, but he came away with some surprising hardware.

"The car won Best of Concourse Factory Original, the Dualgate Award, and the Silver Concourse Award," he said.

"I can't tell you how many guys have come up to me and said I stole the GTO," Bugbee said. "This is from guys who knew about the car before I did.

"All I can say is that they didn't do their homework, and I did."

The Rewards of Persistence

George Garrett of Huntington Beach, California, has always loved the lines of the classic 1939 and 1940 Fords. As a kid, he owned a 1948 Ford, also a good-looking car, but he promised himself that one day he would own and restore a '39 or a '40.

In the mid-1990s, he went to a housewarming party. He was talking to the uncle of the host when he found out they shared an interest in old cars. The man, who was in his mid-seventies, had restored several Model A Fords that had won awards in the AACA and the Model A Restorers' Club of America National meets.

He also mentioned that he had this old 1939 Ford Deluxe coupe that he wasn't quite sure what to do with.

"He was getting older and the thought of tackling another restoration wasn't very appealing to him," Garrett said. "I said I'd like to come out to take a look at the car whenever his schedule allowed, and suddenly his demeanor changed."

Suddenly, the older gentleman began to say things like, "Gee, why would you want to look at it," and "I'm kind of busy and don't really have the time," and "Do you really want to buy it?"

"I told him I didn't know if I wanted to buy it, but I'd just like to see it sometime," Garrett said.

Garrett told the gentleman he'd give him a call the following week and they'd compare their calendars.

But it was excuse after excuse—one week the coupe owner was traveling to San Diego, the next to Santa Barbara, the third week he didn't feel well, and so on and so on.

"I finally called his niece, the host of the party, and she said the cars were his babies, and that she understood his reluctance in showing them," he said. "I decided to drop the issue for a while."

Garrett got busy at work and almost a year had passed when he went to a shopping mall. A sidewalk antique sale was going on. One of the vendors had old car literature and advertisements for sale, categorized by year, make, and model.

George Garrett met an older gentleman at a party and discovered quite by accident that he owned a 1939 Ford coupe. After being told the car was not for sale, he eventually found out it had been sold to another collector. *George Garrett*

As luck would have it, the vendor had a great 1939 Ford Deluxe advertisement that Garrett purchased.

"I went right over to an art supply store and bought some nice museum board and mounted and framed it," he said. "I sent the framed piece to my friend's uncle with a note that I hoped he enjoyed the picture, and reminded him that if he ever wanted to sell the car, to keep me in mind."

After the older gentleman received the gift, he called Garrett.

"I could hear that he was crying, and he thanked me for the gift," Garrett said. "He really appreciated it, and I was already imagining the car sitting in my driveway.

"Then he dropped the bombshell; he told me he had already sold the car."

Garrett was shocked and heartbroken. The gentleman offered to send the gift back, but Garrett refused, saying that the framed print was his to enjoy. But then he heard something that gave him hope. The gentleman had heard that the new owner of the coupe had lost interest, and he gave Garrett his phone number.

"I began to call the guy morning, noon and night, and leave messages on his answering machine, but he never returned my calls," Garrett said. "I began to think that maybe this wasn't meant to be."

Garrett turned his mind to work again and a few months went by. One day the old gentleman called to see whatever happened with the coupe.

"I told him the story of the unreturned phone calls, but told him I'd give it another try," Garrett said. "Wouldn't you know it, but I left another message and the new owner called me back twenty minutes later."

It took forty-five days, but finally Garrett and the coupe's new owner met. The owner had quite a collection of old cars, including a Model T Ford, a Model A Ford, a 1956 Chevy Nomad, a '57 Chrysler, and an old fire truck. And the '39 coupe.

Garrett believes that the new owner's intentions were to quickly get the coupe running and throw a coat of paint on it. But the car was in need of more work than that.

"It had been repainted a number of times with a brush," Garrett said. "It was so dirty, didn't have the right seat, and when I banged on the backrest, a cloud of dust billowed out like there was a sand storm."

But the original instruments were still in place and the owner's manual was still in the glove box.

Upon further inspection, Garrett realized that the car's frame would likely need straightening because the left front wheel was further back than the one on the right side.

"But on the positive side, there wasn't much Bondo, and all the parts were there," he said. "The only thing I could find missing was the driver's side door panel."

Garrett loved the lines of Dearborn's 1939 and 1940 cars, and even though he owned a 1948 Ford, he promised himself that one day he'd own and restore a '39 or '40 Ford.
George Garrett

Despite losing the car once, Garrett ultimately purchased the coupe and completed a total restoration, creating the showstopper you see here. *George Garrett*

Suddenly, it was soul-searching time.

"Let's see, the car was all original, which meant I wouldn't have to correct someone else's mistakes, the price was fair, and I had just gotten a bonus at work, so I had the money," he said. But it was in need of a thorough restoration.

Garrett purchased the coupe, and the rest is history. After sixteen months of hard work and lots of professional help, he was able to take it on its first drive.

"I'm retired now, so I use the coupe almost everyday when I run errands to the post office or Kinko's," he said. "Strangers are always waving at me at intersections, and sometimes a crowd gathers when I'm parked.

"I hope to drive it across the United States on the Lincoln Highway and go all the way to Times Square in New York City."

Barn-Find Bandits

Thirty years ago, Todd Duhnke went snooping around a barn in Glen Ullin, North Dakota, without permission. He was following up on a tip that a nice old car was buried in one of the stalls under a pile of oats.

"I used to travel quite a bit throughout the upper Midwest in a 1976 Ford LTD for the irrigation company that I worked for," Duhnke said. "During those trips, I developed a friendship with a fellow I met in Bismarck who owned several 1950s Fords. One evening while we were admiring this fellow's recently found '57 Ford Fairlane 500 convertible, I commented that I wished I could find a '57 Sunliner convertible."

Duhnke remembered his father's '57 convertible, which was purchased new from Heiser Ford in Milwaukee, when he was a kid during the winter of 1956-1957.

"My friend mentioned that he in fact knew where an exceptionally nice model was tucked in a barn about forty miles outside of town in the middle of nowhere," he said. "He said it was far too nice for his budget. I don't know what got into us that evening, but we decided to drive out to Glen Ullin then and there, and sneak onto the property to have a look for themselves."

The barn seemed abandoned, but they checked the farmhouse first, to make sure it was in fact unoccupied. Once assured that there would be no angry farmer coming after them with a shotgun, they walked toward the barn. With flashlights in hand, they opened the door and peered into the dusty darkness. There, buried about ankle deep in oats, was a black 1957 Ford Sunliner with 36,000 miles on the odometer. The two barn-find bandits spent about an hour inspecting the car. They determined the top and interior were still original and in excellent condition. The engine turned over easily and the body had only minor rust.

Satisfied with their discovery, they decided it was time to drive back to Bismarck. It was 1:30 a.m.

Once he negotiated the deal to buy the car, Todd Duhnke hooked it up to his LTD company car with a rented tow bar. But the seller was reluctant and decided he really didn't want to sell, which led to a sleepless night for both of them.
Todd Duhnke

Back at work the next morning, Duhnke couldn't help but think about his barn find from the previous evening. Later that day, his car-collecting friend called with the name and phone number of the gentleman who owned the farm.

"I called him and lo and behold, he had been laid off from his job just the day before," Duhnke said. "He told me the story of the car; that it had been purchased new by his family and had spent most of its life in dry western North Dakota and Arizona.

"He said he wanted fifteen hundred dollars for the car, which in 1976 was quite a lot of money for a '57 Ford."

Duhnke tried to negotiate, but his offers fell on deaf ears; the owner was firm about his $1,500 price. He finally swallowed hard and agreed to have the money wired to a local bank the next day.

"The owner couldn't believe that I would buy the car sight unseen," Duhnke said. "Of course, I never told him that I had inspected the car quite thoroughly just the night before."

Duhnke's banker promptly sent the money the next morning. But when he tried to arrange a time to complete the sale, the seller was experiencing an extreme case of seller's remorse. He dreaded parting with the car that had been in his family since it was new. But Duhnke could hear the seller's wife in the background hounding her husband to sell the car.

Finally, the seller said he would honor the deal they had made on the phone, but now he wanted $1,700 for the car. Duhnke scraped together another $200 from his friend and made an appointment with the seller to meet at the bank.

"The seller still couldn't believe that I would pay seventeen hundred dollars for a car that he thought I had never seen," he said.

After paying for the car and signing the proper paperwork, Duhnke went to the local U-Haul rental store and installed a bumper hitch onto his 1976 LTD. Then he and his friend drove out to the farm in Glen Ullin.

They pushed the car out of the barn and, for the first time in many years, into the daylight.

"Boy, it looked good," Duhnke said.

Duhnke and his friend disconnected the driveshaft, added air to the bald tires, and readied the car for the long tow home. The seller mentioned that he had four other 1957 Fords on the property, and that Duhnke could pick whatever parts he thought he would need. After about an hour of removing the most desirable items, he nervously drove his LTD, with the '57 hitched behind, back toward Bismarck.

"The car towed fine," Duhnke said. "The first stop we made was at the twenty-five cent car wash to knock off the years of accumulated dirt. The original black paint still shined remarkably well."

His initial concern over spending $1,700 for a nineteen-year-old car quickly evaporated, seeing he had purchased a very nice example.

But when he got back to his hotel, trouble was waiting.

"The guy I bought the car from was waiting for me," Duhnke said. "He said he just couldn't sell the car, and that he was canceling the deal and giving me my money back. Seeing how good the car looked with all the dirt washed off probably made him feel twice as bad.

"I reminded him that we had a legal transaction, and that I wouldn't undo what had been done. Even though his wife was pulling on his arm to leave, he threatened to come back and take the car.

"It was really quite sad because he truly loved the old Ford. I reassured him that I would preserve the car, but also felt that the money I had paid him would help feed his family in light of his job loss. It was obvious he had very limited financial resources."

Feeling somewhat insecure, Duhnke changed his hotel room to one where he could keep his eye on the car overnight. He even asked the hotel staff to watch for anything suspicious and backed the old car up to a tall curb with his Ford LTD blocking it in front.

"I also called the Bismarck police to please keep an eye on the car overnight," he said. "Once they heard my story, and the seller's comments, they were happy to oblige."

At about 11 p.m. that evening, he spotted the seller in his old truck from his hotel room window.

"He parked his truck in the parking lot near where the '57 was parked," he said. "I don't know if he was going to try to 'rescue' the car, or was simply saying goodbye one last time, but I was happy to see the Bismarck police officers come by every thirty minutes or so."

Duhnke finally fell asleep at about 1:30 a.m.

He woke up early the next morning and headed off for Fargo to attend a meeting. He was relieved to leave Bismarck. At a gas station en route to Fargo, a fellow offered Duhnke $3,000 on the spot for his newly purchased convertible, which he politely declined.

After a good night's sleep in Fargo, he drove off toward home in Omaha, Nebraska, about 600 miles away. With only one spare tire, he worried about the bald tires holding up for the long journey, but his worries went unfounded.

"When I got home, my mom and dad were waiting to see my 'new' '57 Ford," Duhnke said. "Mom started to cry, remembering the good times our family had in our original Ford Sunliner."

Today, more than thirty years later, the Ford sits proudly in Duhnke's garage next to several other collector cars, including a 1956 Ford Fairlane Victoria, an eleven thousand–mile 1964 Thunderbird, and a 1969 Chevelle SS396.

"She's had a full frame-up restoration, but I've tried to keep as many original parts as possible," Duhnke said. "The car now has forty-one thousand miles on it and has led a very pampered life.

"And my folks, still with us, still enjoy the occasional ride in the '57."

The Star-Crossed Flaming Rabbit Daytona Coupe

BY PETER BROCK
CONTRIBUTING EDITOR FOR *SPORTS ILLUSTRATED*, *FORZA*,
CORVETTES, *DIRT SPORTS*, AND *AUTO AFICIANADO*.

Old race cars weren't worth much in 1965, even those with considerable history such as Carroll Shelby's six-time world champion Daytona Cobra coupes. For less than the price of a new Austin-Healy, knowledgeable enthusiasts could cruise down to Shelby's race shop on Princeton Drive, near Venice, California, pick out an obsolete team car—complete with its last race numbers and old FIA tech stickers still affixed—and rumble off into the sunset with more power under the hood than a Titan Rocket.

The Daytona coupe prototype known as CSX 2287 had been hurriedly constructed in the Princeton shop in late 1963, just as Carroll Shelby's tiny Ford-backed organization was becoming the leading force in American racing. The unique coupe was the first of the six that made Shelby American a legend in motorsports and gave American racing credibility in international GT racing.

Prior to its first race at Daytona in early 1964, CSX 2287 had been a divisive entity within the team. Hardly anyone in the race shop had any affinity for the oddly-shaped racers, whose stiffer chassis and sleeker lines were designed to propel the coupes past Ferrari's all-conquering 250 GTOs on the world's fastest racing circuits.

Only Ken Miles, Shelby's talented lead driver, had any real confidence in the concept—along with the vision to see where the idea could take the team. Despite resistance from the team's most influential member, Phil Remington, Miles persuaded a dubious Shelby to let a part-time Kiwi mechanic named John Ohlsen—known around the shop as "the kid"—build his car. Since there was no real budget for the project, none of the team's master fabricators were

Freshly built, and still in raw aluminum, Peter Brock's very first Daytona coupe, CSX 2287, sits in the Shelby shop waiting for its first track test at Riverside. The sleek body finally gave the Cobra a speed advantage over the Ferraris. *Peter Brock*

permitted to work on it. Ohlsen, Miles, and I completed the car in just ninety days, finally persuading some of the other team members to help on their own time. The unpainted coupe's first test at Riverside Raceway a few weeks later won over the doubters and made the bizarre-looking racer the focus of Shelby's plans to expand his organization and challenge Enzo Ferrari's supremacy in Europe.

Ironically, the Shelby team was so small at the time that they couldn't build any more Daytona coupes and meet the demands of all the other racing projects that were beginning to gravitate to Shelby's bustling enterprise in Venice. As a result, the other five Daytona coupes were inexpensively bodied for Shelby at Carrozzeria Gransport in Modena, Italy, right under Ferrari's nose.

CSX 2287, the California built prototype, had been run hard and put away wet. As it was the first of the six to hit the track against Enzo's finest, it had more races in its logbook than any of the others. At one time or another, it had been driven by almost every name driver on the Shelby team. This history makes it one of the most important racers ever to come out of Shelby's premises.

In a strange turn, Miles was never permitted to drive the original car or any of the other coupes following the Riverside test. What caused the rift between Shelby and Miles was never discussed publicly, but it lasted throughout their relationship, right up until the time Miles was set to win Le Mans in 1966 and then instructed to hold back on the last lap so another team could win.

That first coupe had been Miles' dream, custom built around his slender frame like a bespoke suit and then, mysteriously, Shelby took it away from him.

In its first race in 1964, driven by Dave McDonald and Bob Holbert, it easily set the Daytona lap record. They led Ricardo Rodriguez and Phil Hill, in the latest Ferrari Type 64 GTO prototype, until a horrendous pit fire sidelined the coupe's effort in the seventh hour. A few weeks later, the duo won the GT category at Sebring, convincing Henry Ford II that the Texan's strange-looking 289-powered coupes might have a chance to beat Ferrari's GTOs. As a result of that watershed twelve-hour win, Ford wrote Shelby the check that ignited the ferocious four-year battle between the Shelby Ford and factory Ferrari teams.

At the Le Mans trials a few weeks later, with Frenchman Jo Schlesser at the helm, CSX 2287 set the weekend's fastest unofficial top speed on the rain-slicked Mulsanne, besting Ford's new GT40s. Both of Ford's new supercars crashed as a result of aerodynamic instability. Then Phil Hill took the lone Daytona and set the lap record with it at Spa, and soon after that the same car led Le Mans for twelve hours, with Chris Amon and Jochen Neerpasch at the wheel. By that time a second coupe had been completed in Modena, and Shelby's Daytonas were running one-two (with Bondurant and Gurney in the second car) until the rattled Ferrari team vehemently protested a questionable Cobra pit stop procedure. Bondurant and Gurney won the GT category for Shelby and Ford in the second coupe, but CSX 2287 might have won the race overall had it not been for the Italians' protest.

The California-built prototype ran nine FIA events during the Texan's two-year campaign against Ferrari and helped scare the flaming bejeezus out of Enzo, who even went so far as to have the last FIA race of the 1964 season, at Monza, cancelled because he knew Shelby was coming with three of his new coupes.

CSX 2287's final hours in late 1965 were spent on the vast Bonneville Salt Flats, where land-speed kings Craig Breedlove and

After its road racing days were over, CSX 2287 was brought to the Bonneville Salt Flats in Utah, where it broke twenty-three international FIA/USAC records with drivers Craig Breedlove and Bobby Tatroe.
Peter Brock

Bobby Tatroe used the old war horse to set twenty-three international USAC/FIA speed records. The Goodyear-sponsored record runs were actually a ruse to keep Firestone-shod challenger Art Arfons and his wickedly fast jet-powered *Green Monster* from upping the ante over Breedlove's similarly-powered *Spirit of America* and Tatroe's rocket-powered *Wingfoot Express*. Both of the Goodyear-backed record breakers were temporarily down for repairs and Arfons was ready to run, threatening to eclipse their times. USAC rules dictated that contestants for world speed records could hold the salt until they were finished, providing they made some sort of record attempt every day.

With Breedlove and Tatroe's cars both on the trailer, Goodyear's PR reps frantically called their West Coast distributor, Shelby, and begged to borrow one of his Daytonas. They figured Breedlove and Tatroe could pretend to set some sort of endurance and speed records while holding the salt. By pure serendipity, a spit-shined CSX 2287 had just returned from Ford's auto show circuit, so Shelby told crew chief Tom Greatorex to install a new engine, mount the largest rear tires available, and head for Utah. Less than eighteen hours later, an exhausted Greatorex arrived at the edge of the famed saline speedway and rolled the old road racer off its trailer . . . just in time to prevent an intense Arfons from taking the salt.

At first only straightaway records were sought, but as the day wore on and the Goodyear team actually began to put some records away, the conspiracy thickened. Why not run for twelve hours? That would hold the salt for another day and if they were lucky a predicted storm front would arrive, flood the track, and Breedlove and Tatroe's records for Goodyear would be safe from Arfon's assault—at least for that year.

A twelve-mile circular course was quickly surveyed, and at dawn the next day, the marathon began. No provisions for refueling had been made, so Greatorex drove into nearby Wendover and purchased several fifty-gallon drums of gasoline and a hand pump to transfer the fuel to the coupe. Around and around they went, hour after hour while the anxious Firestone contingent sat on their hands scanning the horizon for rain. When Breedlove and Tatroe tired of the game, even Greatorex sat in for a stint.

After several hours, the salt had become so rutted that the coupe was literally being shaken to pieces. Duct tape, bailing wire, and hastily installed pop rivets kept the effort going and by sunset the gnarly, salt-brine incrusted Daytona had racked up a 150-mile-per-hour average (including fuel stops), setting a new World's GT endurance record for twelve hours.

When Greatorex returned to Venice, Shelby was aghast at the condition of his once-pristine show car. Rather than spend weeks trying to restore it to show condition, the ever-practical Texan casually offered it to Greatorex for $800.

"Naah, I don't think so," replied the dead-tired crew chief. "I've had enough."

Some weeks later, the now-resuscitated coupe was sold to slot car magnate Jim Russell, whose one-twenty-fourths scale Russkit model of the World Champion coupe was breaking sales records across the nation.

"I paid Shelby forty-five hundred dollars for the car and drove it all over Southern California to promote my model car business. It was the most fun I've ever had in a car," Russell said. "It was fast, noisy, and totally reliable—I really got my money's worth, believe me!"

About a year later, Russell sold the car for $12,500 ("a considerable profit," thought Russell) to famed rock producer, Phil Spector. To impress the unaware, Spector had the doors of his coupe emblazoned with lettering informing the masses that he was driving the "World's Champion," plus an erroneous note below that the Daytona was equipped with a 700-horsepower "427" Ford engine.

The Wall of Sound music impresario didn't know much about cars, but the impression his thunderous arrival at clubs along the Sunset Strip made was pure Hollyweird. Spector is reported to have offended more of L.A.'s finest than was deemed prudent by his business manager who, legend has it, forced him to sell the car after he'd blown the engine in a midnight orgy of speed. It was that or spend considerable time in the gray-bar hotel, so Spector reluctantly parted with his pet rocket for a reported paltry $1,000, selling it to his roadie-friend and house handyman George Brand, who in turn gave it to his daughter Donna and son-in-law John O'Hara.

The O'Haras, who then lived in Richard Nixon's hometown of Yorba Linda, often drove it up to their cabin in the San Bernardino Mountains around Big Bear Lake. In time, the marriage went sour and the couple divorced. Under California's community property law, all assets acquired during a marriage are supposed to be divided equally. Since the car's value was contested by both parties, the judge awarded the car to Mrs. O'Hara, reportedly under the stipulation that when it was sold, half the proceeds would revert to John O'Hara. With no time limit established for its sale, Donna O'Hara

Race car collector Dr. Fred Simeone maneuvered his way past lawyers, lawsuits, friends, and relatives to become the owner of probably the most famous Shelby car ever built. *Tom Cotter*

parked the Daytona at her home in Yorba Linda and refused to speak with anyone regarding its future.

As the years passed and the collector's market gained steam, Cobra enthusiasts from all over the world began to seek out the rarest of Shelby's old racers. The six Daytona coupes, being the most valuable, because of their history, were soon trading for six figures or more. The remaining five coupes had long since been acquired and restored to perfection, where they continued to trade in an ever-escalating market.

Even Shelby, who had long eschewed his old racers, began to understand their true value and located one in Japan that had reportedly belonged to a member of Japan's mysterious mafia. Author and Cobra historian Mike Shoen brokered the deal that returned CSX 2300 to California, where it was rebuilt by famed restoration expert Mike McClusky.

Shelby kept that car for twenty years until it was scammed out from under him in a controversial Las Vegas flim-flam that still has the Texan's blood boiling at mention of the incident. Eventually, Shelby's coupe wound up at auction in Monterey, where it sold for more than four million dollars. That benchmark sent rare car brokers all over the world into frenzy. The finder's fee alone for locating O'Hara's "missing" coupe, CSX 2287, was rumored to be at least $1 million.

Several California Cobra club insiders knew that O'Hara had the car, but no one was able to locate the owner. She was using her own name, but managed to elude almost everyone who attempted to track her down.

The most intense searches ended with the discovery of her parents, George and Dorothy Brand. By this time, George Brand had succumbed to Alzheimer's and was living in an Orange County nursing home. Mrs. Brand was ninety-two years old, living in HUD-subsidized housing near San Diego, and had little contact with her estranged daughter, Donna O'Hara, who had quietly moved to a modest apartment in La Habra and was working as a shipping clerk at Sears.

While O'Hara was in La Habra, the car was stashed in Santa Ana. Some thirty years earlier, she had arranged to place the Daytona in a public storage unit to keep it out of public view. More and more reclusive as time passed, she continued to pay the cost of its sanctuary, even though she was aware of the car's increased value and could have comfortably retired on the profit. Legend has it that she so hated her ex that she refused to sell the car knowing that half the proceeds, by law, would have to go to him.

On October 22, 2000, police in Fullerton were notified of an old, gray-haired woman acting strangely near a suburban horse trail. When they investigated, they found a gruesome sight. The elderly woman, with her two pet rabbits in hand, had doused herself with gasoline and become a human torch. She was still alive when the flames abated, but contentiously refused to reveal her name. She died eleven hours later without ever divulging her identity or the reason for her strange behavior.

Baffled police could only identify her as a homeless "Jane Doe," placing notices in the local press asking for assistance in solving the case and locating possible relatives. It took more than seven weeks before anyone noticed that O'Hara was missing.

One of the people aware of the car's existence was an English rare car broker named Martin Eyears, who was living in Montecito,

California. He had found the car before her death and had tried to purchase it. When he contacted O'Hara's boss at Sears to see if the recluse might consider a revised offer, he was told she had died. Eyears went straight to Dorothy Brand, Donna's elderly mother, and convinced her that as the rightful heir to Donna's property she could sell him the car.

In the meantime, an apparent childhood friend of O'Hara's, Kurt Goss, filed suit in Orange County claiming that he was the rightful owner of the car. Goss, it seems, had a DMV title transfer signed by Donna O'Hara that had been made out just five days prior to her death.

To counter that claim, a cousin of O'Hara's, Charles Jones, stated in other court documents that the DMV title transfer had indeed been found in O'Hara's effects after her death, but that the space indicated for the new owner had been left blank. Jones claims Goss took the document without permission and inserted his own name.

In the meantime, rent had not been paid on the storage facility, so the car was in jeopardy of being auctioned off to the highest bidder for simple storage costs. Eyears and Mrs. Brand arrived, paid off the back rent, and took possession of the coupe.

Mrs. Brand was reportedly paid over $2.2 million for the car at that time. Eyears had made a verbal pre-sale arrangement with Steve Volk, of the nonprofit Shelby Museum in Boulder, Colorado, to resell the car to Volk's museum for $3.75 million. Then Eyears suddenly backed out of that deal and sold the car for a much higher figure to Fred Simeone, a wealthy neurosurgeon, from Philadelphia. The car is now in Simeone's possession in Pennsylvania.

A preliminary hearing on Goss' suit was heard by Orange County's Superior Court Judge James P. Gray on March 6, 2001. The judge was astounded by the litigant's statements, but still agreed that Goss' case had merit. The IRS evidently became involved as well, wanting its cut of the sale.

Mrs. Brand, who had reportedly made tracks for Florida and the Caymans after receiving payment from Eyears, is rumored to have

The Cobra ID plate that had eluded collectors for decades, CSX 2287. *Tom Cotter*

told the IRS that she had given much of the money "to the homeless."

Judge Gray ordered any remaining funds placed in a special trust until the true owner of the car could be established and set a second hearing for April 17, 2001. When that date rolled around, who should show up in Orange County Court but O. J. Simpson's Beverly Hills attorney, Robert Shapiro, representing Phil Spector. Shapiro claimed that Spector, now sixty, never sold the car to his roadie, but simply asked him to store it for him "as an investment." The fact that Spector had never checked on his car once in the thirty-plus years that it was gone didn't seem out of place to Shapiro.

"He's a recluse," said the lawyer. "It's not uncommon for him to entrust his possessions to others for safe keeping until he wants them."

Meanwhile, much of the money that Eyears paid to Brand had disappeared, and someone was going to be out big time before the judge decided if the car should be returned to California to determine its rightful owners. The car just might have been returned to California from Pennsylvania and suffered the tortuous probate procedures that could have taken months or even years, but all ended quietly when Dr. Simeone contacted Goss and paid him an undisclosed sum to sign the title over to him. Goss reportedly also had the key to resolving the other sticky wicket, a bill of sale from Spector to Brand.

End of case.

The Watermelon Man and the Cobra

Editor's note: This article by author Tom Cotter first appeared in the August 2007 issue of Road & Track *magazine.*

In spring 1963, two young men on opposite sides of the country were plying their chosen crafts, each on his way to success. On the West Coast, Carroll Shelby was eager to prove his own brand of sports car—the Cobra—could be successful both on the racetrack and in the showroom.

On the East Coast, a young musician was pounding keyboards and writing songs that he hoped would jump to the top of the jazz charts.

For a brief moment that April, these two men's lives converged.

Even though Shelby's California operation was still in its infancy, his new car's brilliance was already being realized. In February 1963, the Cobra recorded its first win at Riverside Raceway, and then nearly won Daytona and Sebring.

In New York, pianist and composer Herbie Hancock was also quietly celebrating his first success. In the mail that April, Hancock received a check for $3,000 as a royalty payment for his classic tune *Watermelon Man*. To a twenty-two-year-old in 1963, this was a fortune.

For Hancock, who lived in the Bronx and commuted to rehearsals in Manhattan by subway, his first thought was to spend his windfall on a station wagon. After all, he was a musician and he could pack fellow musicians and their instruments in the back. But his roommate, jazz trumpeter Donald Byrd, convinced him otherwise. Byrd drove his girlfriend's Jaguar and was a sports car aficionado. He convinced Hancock to consider a new sports car that was beginning to get attention and had just gone on display in Manhattan.

"Donald told me the Cobra was kicking Ferrari's ass," Hancock said. The next day he hopped on the L train and headed to Charles Kreisler Automobiles on Broadway.

Jazz legend Herbie Hancock took his first royalty check for $3,000 and purchased the sixth AC Cobra ever built, CSX 2006. He used the car as his everyday set of wheels, traveling from New York to gigs in Boston, Detroit, Chicago, and even California.
Herbie Hancock Collection

"I had never bought a car in my life. I had only driven an old Dodge my father bought me for college."

Instead of feeling excited as he walked into the dealership, Hancock experienced racism that, sadly, was all too common in 1963. Even though the civil rights movement was gaining momentum—Dr. Martin Luther King would deliver his famous "I Have A Dream" speech just four months later—that didn't seem to register with the salesman on duty. Noticing the young black man walking into the showroom, the salesman all but ignored Hancock and continued reading his newspaper.

"I walked right up to his desk and asked if I could see the Cobra," Hancock said, admitting that he was shabbily dressed. "He never looked up or answered my questions. He just pointed in the direction of the car. "

Hancock attempted to engage the salesman in conversation about the Cobra's specifications and features, but no luck.

"He pissed me off," he said.

Hancock walked across the showroom to CSX 2006, the sixth production Cobra ever built. He was instantly smitten. It was Old English White, with a red leather interior and silver wire wheels. Under the hood was a high-performance 245-horsepower 260-cubic-inch engine that had originally been developed for the Fairlane. Interestingly, it is the only known Cobra ever equipped with a two-barrel carburetor.

"I walked up to it and kicked the tires, because that's what I heard you were supposed to do," he said, upset over the salesman's attitude.

"I walked back to his desk and said, 'OK, I want to buy it.'"

Hearing that, the salesman suddenly lifted his eyes and asked, "Do you have any idea how much that car costs?"

"Yeah, six thousand dollars. I'll be back tomorrow to pick it up," said Hancock, who admits that he probably would not have purchased the Cobra if the salesman hadn't been so rude.

Eventually Hancock moved to California and bought a Ferrari. But he still owns CSX 2006 and remains the longest original owner of a Cobra in the world besides Carroll Shelby himself. *Tim Considine*

The next day, his friend Byrd accompanied him to pick up the new car. This time Hancock was dressed in a suit. Word of his celebrity had apparently spread throughout the dealership because this time he was treated like royalty. He paid $2,500 in cash, and financed the balance through the dealership. He was nervous about the performance of his new purchase.

"That car could go from zero to a hundred in less than a block," he said. That acceleration, plus a very stiff clutch pedal, convinced Hancock that his friend Byrd should drive the car back to the Bronx.

"I rented a garage for the car near Donald's house, but didn't drive it for the first two weeks because I was scared," he said.

"But everyday I'd sit in the car and press the clutch . . . and make motor noises with my mouth," he said with a laugh.

Finally, as Hancock became more comfortable with the Cobra, he began taking it out for short drives. One day several weeks after his purchase, Byrd was involved in a minor accident while driving the Cobra.

"'Herbie, I screwed up your car,' he said to me on the phone. I said, 'Hey, man, don't worry about it; it's just a car.'

"That fender bender connected me to reality."

From that time on, CSX 2006 was no longer a shrine, but a daily driver. As soon as it left the body shop, Hancock began driving it to gigs in Philadelphia, Boston, and Chicago, and even drove it to California a couple of times. Hancock chalked up more than seventy thousand miles on the Cobra before the speedometer cable broke.

Eventually, Hancock moved to California and began using the Cobra less and less. He purchased a new Ferrari in 1990, and CSX 2006 was put in storage.

"When I bought the Ferrari, I went into the garage and had a long talk with the Cobra," Hancock said. "I said, 'This is for your own good; you're too valuable to drive. Look, I'm replacing you with a Ferrari; at least it's not a Chevy.'"

In April 2006, the sixty-six-year-old Hancock celebrated his forty-third year of Cobra ownership. The only person who has owned a Cobra for a longer span of time is Carroll Shelby, who still owns prototype CSX 2000.

Both Shelby and Hancock went on to become hugely successful. Shelby's cars won an untold number of races and championships. Hancock has written scores of hits and chart-busting albums. But despite these accolades, Hancock remains passionate towards his four-wheeled companion.

"I'll never sell it," he said. "It represents my first success in life."

CHAPTER FIVE

The Luck of the Car Hunters

Between the Devin and the Deep Blue Sea

BY PAUL DUCHENE, MANAGING EDITOR, *SPORTS CAR MARKET*

If a desirable barn find is the closest a car buff gets to God, as Peter Egan said, then Tom Shaughnessy must be the Almighty's riding mechanic right now.

California collector Shaughnessy scored a genuine 1952 Ferrari 340 America Spider chassis this summer in a Frankfort, Illinois, garage sale. The sale was on eBay and Shaughnessy bought it for

Before falling into obscurity and disrepair, Chassis No. 0202 A, a 1952 340 America, was campaigned at a number of significant races, including the 1952 24 Hours of Le Mans, before being sold to Luigi Chinetti in 1953. *Tom Shaughnessy Collection*

$26,912—less than one percent of the car's estimated restored value.

In a story full of twists, both he and seller Mike Sanfilippo are delighted with the outcome of the auction and the seller plans to be on hand when the restored car is presented to the world. Shaughnessy hopes to have a running, driving chassis as soon as next summer. A correct body will follow.

"I got tired of pushing it around my shop and built a wooden shelf to get it out of the way," said the cheery Sanfilippo, a retired drag racer who used to run a blown, injected 1960s front-engine car. "I almost cut up the chassis to make a hot wheels dragster out of the Devin body. Good thing that goofy project never happened!"

Sanfilippo replied to condolences (presumably from underbidders) on the Ferrari chat page with breezy cheer. He embraces the profound idea that no one owns historic artifacts; instead they simply become chapters in the provenance.

Ernie McAfee purchased the car from Chinetti and owned it until 1958. The next owner installed a Chevy V-8. Afterwards, an accident had the owner install a Devin fiberglass body. *Andy Herron*

"What's with you guys?" he wrote. "I'm getting more condolences than congratulations. I paid two hundred dollars over fifteen years ago and have no idea of how to restore it properly. That's a thirteen thousand five hundred percent return on my investment in fifteen years. Not bad in my book!"

You can make the case that this might be the best barn find to date. It's certainly up there with the Figoni and Falaschi–bodied Delahaye 135M that was dragged out of Czechoslovakia and restored to win the Pebble Beach Concours d'Elegance.

Shaughnessy's bargain is a case of the smart bird getting the worm, as thousands of collectors had the same opportunity to identify the chassis. It carried a Devin fiberglass body for the last forty-six years, leading to confusion over its origins. Sanfilippo thought it might be a prototype Devin SS and said he was really trying to sell the Devin body and just giving the frame away.

"Lots of guys were going to come and see it, but only one did," said Sanfilippo, who dismantled the car for a thorough series of

Chicago drag racer Mike Sanfilippo bought chassis No. 0202 A as a clapped-out shell for $200 in 1990 with the intention of installing a supercharged big-block engine. Thankfully, he never found the time to convert the car for quarter-mile action. *Tom Shaughnessy Collection*

Still wearing its prancing horse badge, the fiberglass Ferrari languished in Sanfilippo's garage until he decided to list it on eBay in 2006. *Tom Shaughnessy Collection*

photographs and answered numerous e-mail queries from the United States and Europe.

Early Ferrari expert Hilary Rabb examined the car closely once Shaughnessy had bought it, and made a surprising discovery. The chassis revealed the number 0202 A, making Shaughnessy's buy even sweeter, and he doubled his tipster's finder's fee to $20,000.

Because it is an even-number chassis, this is a factory competition car, one of 475 made between 1948 and 1974, almost all of which are accounted for. (In case you want to check your own barn, the numbers range from 0002–0896 and 1002–1050).

Shaughnessy was prepared to go as high as $264,000 if somebody else recognized 0202 A, but when the auction closed June 20, he had won the car for one percent of its restored value, Swiss Ferrari expert Marcel Massini estimated.

The chassis is one of twenty-five 340 Americas built. Nine were bodied by Touring, eleven by Vignale (this is one), and five by Ghia. Sister cars to this are 0196 A and 0204 A. A full restoration is planned in cooperation with the Ferrari factory in Maranello, which has just formed a Classiche Division to authenticate vintage Ferraris.

"While we were bidding, we deduced the car had to be between number 150 and number 260, based on the steering box and spring and shock locations," Shaughnessy said. "We knew it wasn't a Farina car; we knew it had to be Vignale or Touring. The vented brakes should have told us. Marcel hit the nail on the head."

Massini has tracked the history of 0202 A, and it makes for exciting reading. The car raced at the 1952 Le Mans with Maurice Trintignant and Louis Rosier, but did not finish. The factory then loaned it to Piero Scotti, who ran several significant races and won three important hillclimbs. Other racers borrowed it until U.S. importer Luigi Chinetti bought it in 1953 and reportedly sold it to Ernie McAfee in Los Angeles. He owned it until 1958, then sold 0202 A to Paul Owens in Houston, who installed a Chevrolet V-8.

Worse was to follow. After a crash in which the passenger was killed, a Devin fiberglass body was fitted and the resulting combination advertised in *Sports Car* magazine for $4,250. The car's next stop was Utah in 1963; it later made its way to the Chicago area and Sanfilippo bought it in about 1990.

"I heard about it and the guy wanted two hundred dollars. His kid had abandoned it in his garage. I took my trailer and picked it up. I bought it for the cool body," he recalled. "I thought, how cool would it be to have a big-block, blown Ferrari drag car?"

Millions of eBay users had the opportunity to purchase this car, but only collector Tom Shaughnessy recognized the Ferrari chassis, wheels, suspension, and brakes . . . and the all-important serial number stamped into the chassis. Even though he was prepared to bid as much as $264,000 for the car, he paid $26,912. *Tom Shaughnessy Collection*

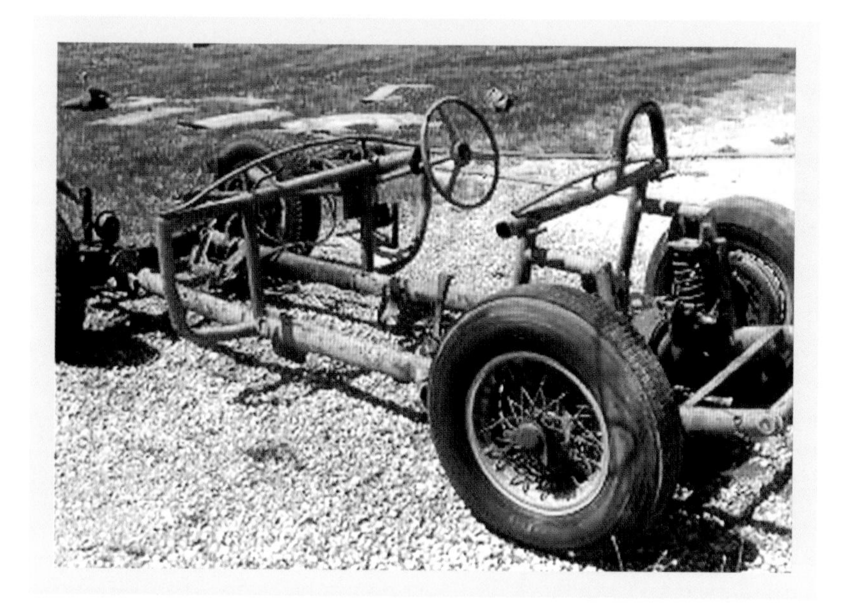

Of course Shaughnessy's purchase price is just a down payment on what it will cost to restore 0202 A. The front part of the chassis is intact, though the front spring is missing. The center section and rear have been modified with the rear leaf spring mounts cut off. But the brakes are complete and the axles and wheels are correct.

Shaughnessy reckons a neophyte who dropped off the chassis at a professional restoration shop could end up writing a check for seven figures—still acceptable, considering the completed value.

Shaughnessy thinks a capable restorer who knows what he is doing will still have to spend between $500,000 and $600,000.

"A 340 motor will cost $200,000, transmission $25,000, differential $20,000, chassis preparation and repair $100,000, and a new body about $200,000," he said.

And here's where Shaughnessy has the edge. "This car went to the best guy in the world to have it," he said. "I already have a running engine, rear end, transmission, pedal box, radiator, and oil cooler. I have half the car."

He even thinks he knows where the original V-12 engine is and hopes he can persuade the present owner to trade for his motor, which is close to the same number.

"I'm pleased as punch," he said. "There are four pages on the Ferrari chat online and that enthusiasm is part of car culture. I'll have to put a sticker on the back, 'I bought it on eBay.'"

In the way that everything happens at once, Shaughnessy had just bought a Ferrari 375 and scrambled to cover the cost (however modest) of his latest project.

"I wholesaled a Porsche and drove across town to put a check in the bank," he said.

Shaughnessy was worried how Sanfilippo would react to inevitable comments that he should have held out for more money, but Sanfilippo wrote to Shaughnessy to reassure him.

"Tom was concerned about my response, but I'm good with this," Sanfilippo said. "I told him I don't have the knowledge, the resources, or the contacts to restore the car properly. I'm totally excited it went to the right person. This car's been missing for forty-three years. Let's just be happy it's back."

This Triumph Was Almost Overlooked

STORY AND PHOTOS BY TIM SUDDARD, PUBLISHER OF *CLASSIC MOTORSPORTS* AND *GRASSROOTS MOTORSPORTS*

The internet has changed the dynamics of finding cool old cars in barns. In the old days, your finds were relatively easy to keep secret. In the world of instant access and car club internet activity, most finds will almost instantly be known to the enthusiast community.

This can work for you or against you, depending on how you use this power.

I woke up one Saturday morning in the fall of 2005 and my e-mail inbox was all a-buzz. The Friends Of Triumph (FOT), an internet group of Triumph racers that I belong to, were all talking about a local classified ad that one of the members had found. A Triumph GT6 was up for sale in a rural southern Virginia *Auto Trader* or *Pennysaver*.

The car was reputed to be an old Group 44 race car. In the world of British car collecting, Group 44 is the Holy Grail. Bob Tullius' Group 44 race team was the primary factory-backed team, first for Triumph, then MGB and Jaguar when the three companies merged in the late sixties.

The internet buzz turned negative as several members of the FOT posted that they thought the car was a fake. The concerns were raised due to the fact that the build date for the car was July 1969, which means the car was built halfway through the racing season. How could this be the car that Group 44 campaigned for the 1969 season?

While most of the internet group dismissed the car as a fake, I decided to do a little more research. I had met Lanky Foushee, who worked as Group 44's crew chief until the team disbanded in the 1990s. After another quick internet search, I realized that Lanky lived only ninety-three miles from where the car was located. I called Lanky, and he remembered me.

As the unofficial historian of these cars, he was also willing to go take a look at the offering. I asked him about the suspect build date on the car, and he explained that the original car was wrecked so badly at an event at Nelson Ledges that summer that the entire car had to be rebuilt in a week for the next event, starting with a new "body in white" from the factory. He also explained that if this was the same car, it was the car that Mike Downs took to an SCCA National Championship in November of 1969 at Daytona International Speedway.

With this kind of history, even in its current clapped-out condition, this Triumph GT6 race car could be worth ten times more than the average $2,000 to $3,000 paid for old race cars. Restored, a car like this could be worth between $50,000 and $100,000 in today's crazy market.

Lanky's report came back positive. Despite an ugly blue repaint, he recognized it as one of his own as soon as he got within ten feet of the old GT6.

When I went to pick the car up, I stopped at Lanky's shop and asked him to give us a walk around the car, in which he carefuly I

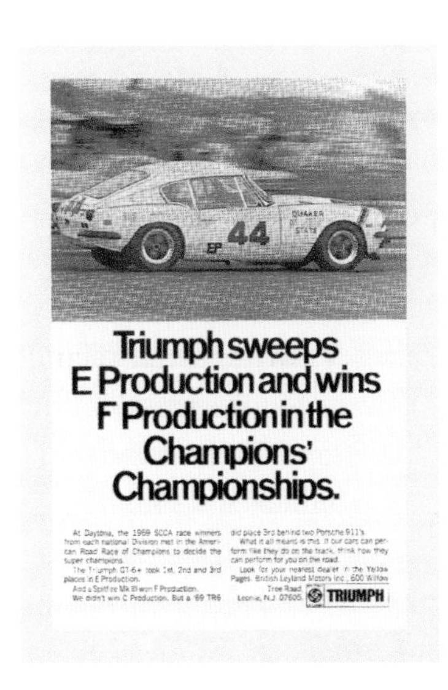

Triumph was so pleased with the Group 44 GT6s' performance that it ran a national advertisement. The GT6s claimed first, second, and third in the 1969 Road Race of Champions. *Tim Suddard Collection*

explained all the tips and tricks that made him realize that this was the same car.

Subsequent research with the Triumph Society of America—the factory-backed club for Triumph owners when the company was still in business—unearthed a photograph of the original car being hit on track at Nelson Ledges. The accompanying text explained that a new body was needed to rebuild the car in a week for its next race.

Unfortunately, the owner knew the car was real and knew what a car with this type of race history was worth. We paid $12,000 on an asking price of $15,000. While this was four to five times what an old Triumph race car with no history would probably sell for, we just had to save this car.

Once home, upon closer inspection, we found the Triumph to be in very good condition. No rust and no major accident damage were found. These are the two things that make restoration so difficult.

As the owner of *Classic Motorsports* and *Grassroots Motorsports,* I plan to restore the car and write about it on the pages of our magazines. Again using the power of the internet, you can follow along, as we have already posted updates and photos at www.ClassicMotorsports.net.

Triumph collectors disregarded the GT6 in the *Auto Trader* ads because the chassis number didn't jive with their records. Tim Suddard was the only one to dig further and learn that a midseason wreck accounted for this car's late production date.
Tim Suddard

The Greatest Barn Find Story Ever Told

Larry Fisette is not a bragger. He's a solid Midwesterner with solid Midwestern values, which include not boasting about your deeds. Yet for those of us who dream of stumbling across the ultimate barn find before our time runs out, sit down and hold on as you read his story.

The sixty-six-year-old Fisette owns a modest auto repair shop and restoration business in De Pere, Wisconsin—not exactly the focal point of the antique car world. If you go to his website (www.depereautocenter.com), you'll see some of the special interest cars he sells. But you'll only find a small reference of the "find" that once had the old car world buzzing, and consumed nearly one year of his life.

"I've been chasing old cars my whole life," Fisette said. "I'm as big an old car guy as you can be."

As an old car aficionado, Fisette would frequent car shows and flea markets. Occasionally at these shows, he would see a gentleman named Don Schlag.

"I had heard of this guy since I moved here in 1969," said Fisette, whose own collection includes a Crosley Hot Shot and a 1959 fuel-injected Impala. "I'd see him at swap meets and we'd say 'Hi,' but not much beyond that."

But Fisette had heard from fellow enthusiasts that the never-married Schlag dedicated his life to scrounging parts. He was, in fact, a mega-collector who had a passion for big-block and high-performance Chevrolet products, and he had quite a stash hidden from public view.

Schlag began to collect high-performance cars and parts many years ago. At first, he would stash the parts in his home garage. When the garage began brimming with parts, he started to move parts into the house. As his passion for collecting grew beyond the

When Larry Fisette committed to buy the late Don Schlag's collection of high-performance Chevy cars and parts, he had no idea what he was dealing with. Twenty-one tractor-trailers were stacked floor to ceiling with tens of thousands of rare parts and fourteen exceptional cars. *Larry Fisette*

house, he used the back of his father's John Deere and implement dealership—Green Bay Equipment—to store the cars and parts he was constantly dragging home. He even made an annual month-long trip to California, where he towed a box trailer behind his motorhome so that he could bring home his purchases.

"Don started buying out old inventory at Chevy dealerships in this area, then he started traveling west every year," Fisette said.

Schlag also developed quite a business during the fuel crisis in the 1970s when the public had no appetite for big-block, gas-guzzling cars stacking up on Chevy dealership lots. Schlag would pick up the big-block cars from the dealerships and bring them to his father's dealership, where he would pull the 427-or 454-cubic-inch engines and substitute them for more fuel-efficient small-block engines. He would then keep the larger engine and charge the dealership $100 to boot!

What drove Schlag to collect these items—during a time when the public had no stomach for such machines—is indeed curious. Was he a "hoarder" of these curious high-horsepower components, or did he in fact suspect that one day the public would again salivate over everything related to the muscle car era?

Schlag wasn't an exclusive parts collector; he occasionally bought cars as well. Fisette once heard that Schlag bought an authentic Yenko Camaro for $1,250 in 1970.

A typical view inside one of the trailers showed that Schlag preserved all types of Chevy parts, from wheels and crankshafts, to transmissions and complete engines. *Larry Fisette*

"I didn't have twelve hundred and fifty dollars for any car that my wife couldn't drive in 1970," Fisette said.

Nobody was quite sure of what cars Schlag had because he was so reclusive.

Two events led to Schlag's reclusivness: His father died in the early 1970s and the family's retail dealership was liquidated; and a fellow enthusiast stole a rare part from Schlag's collection.

Schlag began moving his cars and parts into forty-eight-foot trailers, and when each trailer was full, he would weld up the doors and back another trailer directly against the doors, making them impossible to open.

He even stopped driving his prized Corvettes when one was once "keyed" in a parking lot. He stored those, too, but only after he performed an odd transplant on each. Schlag would swap the engines from car to car, thereby taking the correct numbers-matching engines out of each car. It is believed that Schlag performed this ritual in an effort to make the cars less desirable to thieves.

Cars were also parked nose to tail in the welded-shut trailers. Here is one of the rarest cars in the purchase, an authentic 1969 Yenko Camaro. *Larry Fisette*

One day the rumor that Don Schlag had died began circulating among enthusiasts.

"I heard that he died, so I called his sister and left a message," Fisette said. "I said that I would like to buy the entire collection and then properly manage a liquidation sale.

"I said I would only call once and leave a message. I had given up hope when about four months later I was driving back from our cabin and I received a call from Don's sister. She said she and her children had done a background check on me, and that I was chosen to buy the collection, that I was the one she trusted."

Fisette had no idea what he had committed to. He met the sister, Joanne Stepien, at her deceased brother's house, and they started to clear out the garage. The contents included two Corvettes in addition to loads of parts. After finishing with the garage, they moved on to the closets, the dining room, the kitchen, and the bathrooms. He made an offer for those parts and felt quite satisfied with his good fortune.

"When we thought we had the house completely cleaned out, we made one more sweep through and found a couple more items," Fisette said. "A set of Ed Pink cylinder heads and a fuel injection unit for a 1957 Pontiac."

Then the sister asked if he'd like to start on the rest of the collection.

There was more?

Lots more. Twenty-one tractor-trailer loads more.

"We emptied out the first trailer and spread the items across a warehouse floor," Fisette said. "Stepien's son and I each came up with the value of each trailer. They were very, very fair. It was a trusting deal on both sides."

The first trailer contained two 1970 LS-6 Chevelles parked nose to tail. One was a gold, four-speed bench seat car and the other was an automatic bucket-seat model. Then he stumbled on the aforementioned 1969 Yenko Camaro. A total of fourteen cars were uncovered, including two fuel-injected 1957 Corvettes, a 1963 split window Corvette coupe, a 1964 fuel-injected Corvette roadster, a 1967 435-horsepower Corvette roadster, a 1967 RS/SS Camaro, and a 1972 Z/28 Camaro.

To list the tens of thousands of parts that Fisette purchased from the locked trailers would take up half this book, but highlights include: an experimental fuel injection for a big-block Chevy, brand-new factory side exhausts for Corvettes, a cast-iron COPO 427 engine block, new knock-off Corvette wheels, and even a Yenko hubcap. Fifty-five gallon drums were filled with crankshafts and performance cylinder heads.

Fisette unearthed more than 150 high-performance engines, including six 1969 Z/28 DZ-302 engines, complete down to the breather.

When word of Fisette's discovery began circulating among enthusiasts, the phone at De Pere Auto Center started ringing off the hook. It was all he and his staff could do just to answer the phone from opening to closing each day.

"We had our four phone lines lit for ten straight days," he said. "We could hardly conduct business."

"On one day, I had two hundred and fifty cars in my parking lot and five hundred people walking around the warehouse I rented, and they all wanted something that I had."

One day Fisette hauled seven car loads of people from the airport to the 14,000-square-foot warehouse. In his sincere Midwestern way, he transported the visitors, made hotel reservations, and suggested restaurants.

Was it tiring for Fisette? Hardly.

"I hated to go to bed and couldn't wait to wake up," he said. "I now have friends from all over the country that I'd like to have a beer with."

He had offers coming in from all over the country and around the world. He considered splitting up the collection, which could have become a full-time career selling the pieces on eBay, but decided against it.

"I'm sixty-six years old," he said. "It would have taken me ten years to sell everything. I don't have that much time. But if I were younger, I would have kept everything. I would have restored every

A rare piece of history, the fan shroud on the Camaro still has the original Yenko decal applied. *Larry Fisette*

Here a 1963 Corvette Stingray split-window coupe is pushed from its trailer-tomb. *Larry Fisette*

car and sold every part individually. It interfered with our regular business because all the parts and cars were a business in itself."

In the end, Fisette chose to sell the entire collection to one individual, collector Scott Milestone of Maryland, who already owns a sizable car collection. Fisette sold every single part, down to the last pushrod.

"The buyer had five guys loading the parts into trailers nine hours a day, and it took two weeks. You have no idea how much there was," he said.

"As the truck was pulling out, I saw that a pushrod we used to hold an electrical cord was still in place. I ran outside and gave it to them. I promised I'd sell him everything."

Milestone feels privileged and lucky to have been chosen as the next caretaker of the immense muscle car find.

"Not many people would have been in the position to buy the entire collection," said Milestone, who has purchased several large collections over the years. "Over time, I'll begin breaking up the parts and cars and selling them."

Fisette wishes Milestone well.

After being cleaned up, eight of the fourteen cars were removed from Schlag's trailers. Collectors flew from around the country to view the stash that Fisette had acquired. *Larry Fisette*

"I hope he does as well as I did when he sells the collection because he deserves it," he said.

During the nearly one year of living with one of the largest Chevy barn finds in history, Fisette feels he learned something about Don Schlag.

"I kind of got into his skin," Fisette said. "He had to have been a visionary."

"I think he had a grand plan to one day have a warehouse and be able to see all his stuff lined up. But he died before he could get that accomplished."

Fisette knows exactly the feeling. When he had the thousands and thousands of parts lined up in two rented warehouses—along with the fourteen rare cars—he had an odd feeling of power and accomplishment.

Fisette has had many memorable experiences in the old car business, like the time entertainer Jay Leno—who was performing at a nearby casino—stopped in De Pere Auto Center to look at a supercharged Kaiser that was sitting on the lot. That chance visit began a friendship that continues today.

Once Fisette removed, inventoried, and stored the parts in a rented warehouse, the enormity of the purchase became apparent. More than 150 engines and rare factory fuel injection units were included. *Larry Fisette*

But he said nothing comes close to the barn find.

Did Fisette have a favorite car or a favorite part that he would have like to have kept?

"The Yenko Camaro was my favorite car," he said. "I had an offer of two hundred thousand dollars for that car alone. But I also fell in love with some of the rare parts: big brakes for solid-axle Corvettes, for instance, which were installed on cars that were built for racing. These had metallic linings, and when the cars were used on the street, they didn't work well, so they were usually taken off and discarded. A set of those are probably worth twenty-five thousand to thirty thousand dollars."

"Then there were all the fuel-injection units, factory aluminum cylinder heads, and big gas tanks for 1960 Corvettes. There were all sorts of parts you couldn't buy, no matter how much money you had."

These days, life is much calmer. No more fielding phone calls from around the world and no more runs to the airport to pick up potential buyers. Fisette is back to repairing cars and hunting for more hidden treasure.

He has spoken to a number of people about liquidating their collections, but most he's not interested in.

"These days, nobody wants a trailer of Model A Ford parts," he said.

But he is excited about another pending deal.

"I've been working on it for six months," he said. "If it happens, the thirty-five- to forty-car collection and parts will surpass the Schlag deal."

But Fisette is not pushing. He's made his one phone call and will sit back and wait. It's what Midwesterners do.

High School Hot Rod

Rob Gibby bought a 1930 Model A Ford coupe in 1956 on his fourteenth birthday, exactly fifty years before this story was written. It was bone stock and he paid fifty dollars for it.

"My dad took me to a junkyard in New Jersey," said Gibby, who turned sixty-four in 2006.

"They gave it a push start with a crane, and it started right up. I drove it home from there."

Gibby started to tinker with his new purchase, not really knowing what he was doing. But by 1958, he knew the hot setup for his coupe would be to install a small-block Chevy V-8.

"So my Dad brought me to a junkyard in Perth Amboy, New Jersey, and we bought a 265-cubic-inch engine and transmission right out of a wrecked 1955 Chevy for two hundred fifty dollars," he said.

"I started to install it, but did everything wrong," he said. "So my father met an old Indianapolis mechanic—Johnny Matera, as I remember—and he completed the installation."

Gibby was meticulous in his record keeping. He kept a log of all his purchases, including a 1937 Buick transmission, a 1940 Ford rear end, and a 1949 Studebaker truck dashboard.

"My dad invested twenty-eight hundred dollars into that coupe, which was a lot of money in the 1950s," said Gibby. But his father justified it as keeping his son out of trouble and off the streets. Rob's father did the same for his older brother, although his passion was sports.

Alas, though, the car was sold in 1960 when Rob went off to college. He put his car hobby on hold for many years, as he began dating and then got married. He sold the coupe for $300 and bought a VW.

Decades passed. In 1987, Gibby's life took a shift.

"I got divorced and picked up this car hobby with a vengeance," he said.

Rob Gibby (driving) purchased a stock Model A Ford for $50 on his fourteenth birthday in 1956. With the help of his dad and the local junkyard, he installed a Chevy engine and had the coolest hot rod in high school. *Rob Gibby*

He bought a Model A Ford woody wagon and restored it. He built another Model A woody into a hot rod. His mind turned to the old coupe he had in high school, and he wondered if it still existed. Nearly forty years later, he kept a small black-and-white photo of his coupe on the top of his dresser.

As a member of the National Street Rod Association, he was entitled to a free ad in the membership magazine *Street Scene*. For kicks, he ran a "wanted" ad in one issue in 1999.

"I sent in the ad and promptly forgot about it, " he said. "Nobody's going to read it anyway. What the hell? At the very most, I was hoping to hear from some guy who would say, 'Yeah, I owned it, and crashed it into a tree twenty years ago."

Then one day his new wife called him at the office and asked if he was looking to buy another Model A. Apparently someone named Paul Adams had called and asked if Gibby was interested in his Model A.

Nobody was more surprised with the phone call than Gibby.

"I live in Connecticut now, and I couldn't believe when the guy who called lived just twenty minutes away. Apparently Adams bought the car in 1996 from a guy in New Jersey who purchased it out of a barn in 1965. Since purchasing the coupe, Adams had built the car into a nice 1990s hot rod, according to Gibby. The car had a 350-350, air conditioning, and a new Rod Shop chassis.

"I started to question the guy with details that I remembered like it was yesterday. I asked him about the pedals, whether they were hanging or came up from the floor," Gibby said. "The guy who had the car said the pedals were hanging and had come from a 1956 Ford. Then that's not my car, because I installed Chevy pedals in my coupe.

This is how Gibby's Model A looked when he repurchased it almost forty years later. It was equipped with a modern drivetrain and air conditioning. Gibby is now rebuilding the car to the same condition as when he drove the car to school in Perth Amboy, New Jersey. *Rob Gibby*

"But then I went back to my old logbook and looked it up. Son-of-a-gun, there it was in my own handwriting: 1954 Ford Pedal Assembly from Horbaly's Junkyard, $5.50. I had found my car!"

Now he felt he had to purchase the car, until the owner told him how much money he wanted.

"He wanted fourteen thousand dollars," Gibby said. "Well, that was way too much. But hey, it was neat. I found my old car, but I told him no thanks. I wasn't about to spend fourteen thousand dollars."

The new owner of the coupe, though, really wanted Gibby to have his old car again, so they worked out a deal. The owner of the car would take off all the "modern" parts and pieces, and sell the rest to Gibby. Gibby didn't have any interest in the newer hot rod parts, since his intention was to build the car back to its 1959 condition.

"I was just going to throw it together, but when I was at Hershey that year, a friend convinced me to rebuild it exactly the way I had it in high school," Gibby said, "because then I could display it at Hershey."

So today, Gibby is in the middle of a full restoration of his old hot rod.

"I've changed just a couple of things, like I boxed the chassis because I remember when I really got on the gas in the old days, one headlight would point up in the air."

"Otherwise, I'm going back to the way it was; flex-tube exhaust pipe and black Rustoleum paint on the body."

"I'm having more fun than I've ever had in my life," he said. "I may have a sixty-four-year-old body, but I'm a seventeen-year-old in my mind."

A Nose For Rare Vettes

1954 Corvette

Joe Trybulec really likes unusual Corvettes. The retired Wal-Mart executive has owned many of the iconic sports cars and rattles off the story of one that he's particularly proud of. He was reading a copy of *Hemmings Motor News* in 2000, when a particular ad caught his eye:

"1954 Corvette, 15,000 miles, one owner, fuel-injected V-8 engine."

"Nobody paid attention to the ad because it was listed with fuel injection," said Trybulec of Batesville, Arkansas. He said that the normally desirable six-cylinder car was overlooked by Corvette collectors because they imagined it was some cobbled-up hot rod.

According to Trybulec's research, nothing could have been further from the truth.

Back in 1957, Eb Rose became a factory sports car driver for Chevrolet, hired by then General Motors President Ed Cole. This came about because Rose's father owned Rose Trucking in Houston, and his father had just purchased one hundred new Chevrolet trucks for his business. To show his appreciation to the family, Cole flew down to Texas to eat dinner at the Rose family ranch, which ironically was next to the racing Foyt family's ranch. During dinner, Cole discovered that the younger Rose was tearing up the sprint car circuit in Texas and offered him a driving contract on the spot.

Not long afterward, Cole received word from the Automobile Manufacturer's Association (AMA) that GM, as well as all other U.S. car makers, were required to cease racing activities, disband the teams, and sell the cars and equipment immediately.

Up to that point, Chevrolet's racing program had been managed by an Atlanta-based division called the Southern Engineering and Development Corporation (SEDCO). It provided Chevy with many of the same services that Peter DePaolo, and later Holman-Moody, gave Ford.

Joe Trybulec's 1957 Corvette was one of the most sought-after Corvettes on the planet. As a factory-built racer, the car competed at Daytona, Sebring, and Nassau. *Joe Trybulec Collection*

When the order came to sell the cars, drivers and teams who had been loyal to Chevy had the first opportunity to purchase the equipment. Eb Rose made out like a bandit.

Rose, who had been a factory sports car driver for GM for only a short time, purchased one of the Bill Mitchell SRII race cars and two production-bodied 1957 Corvettes—which had actually raced at Sebring—for the grand total of three dollars. These Vettes had state-of-the-art Black Widow fuel-injected 283 engines built for Sebring, experimental four-speed T10 gearboxes and 4.11:1 rear ends.

Soon thereafter, while racing one of the stock-bodied '57s in Louisiana, Rose crashed and was terribly hurt. The wrecked race car was shipped back to Houston and put in storage at Rose's ranch.

Eventually Eb Rose's friend, George Moore—who owned a three-year-old 1954 Corvette—asked if he could have some of the old parts from the wrecked race car.

"Sure," Rose said. "I only paid a dollar for it."

So Moore transplanted the Sebring racing drivetrain into his

In a rare, but poor-quality photo, here is Trybulec's Corvette (hood up) in a former airplane hangar that served as Chevy's race shop during the 1957 Sebring 12-Hour race. *Joe Trybulec Collection*

six-cylinder 1954, and for a little while must have had the fastest 1954 Corvette on the planet. Soon thereafter, though, George Moore's son took the car to work one day at Shell Oil Company, got into an accident, and damaged the car.

The car was brought back to the Moore's garage, where it sat for the next thirty years.

Trybulec purchased the car out of the *Hemmings* ad, and found he was the only interested party. He suspected the car's drivetrain had an interesting history, and when he called his friend Ken Kayser, an engineer who had worked at the Totowanda engine plant for thirty-five years, he was able to positively identify the drivetrain throughout components as having had Sebring heritage.

"The '54 sits in my garage with fifteen thousand miles on it, untouched from the day I purchased it," Trybulec said. He is clearly proud of his time capsule.

But the '54 Corvette is not the car he is most excited about. Trybulec gets downright giddy when he discusses his really rare find.

After racing was halted because of the 1957 AMA ban, the former Corvette was converted to a street car, painted, and sold to a couple who lived in Chicago. Here it is pictured in a Florida driveway.
Joe Trybulec Collection

1957 Corvette

One day, Trybulec's retired engineer friend Ken Kayser called.

"A car has surfaced in Chicago," he said. "I've been asked to identify it. The owner had a major stroke and his son and daughter need to sell the house and the cars. There is a Corvette in the garage that hasn't moved in forty-six years."

What Kayser discovered was even more amazing than the 1954 Corvette.

The car's owner, Erwin Rohrer, had been an engineer for Rockwell. He was also a friend of renowned GM designer Harley Earl, as well as GM President Ed Cole.

He also loved racing.

One day Cole gave his friend Rohrer a call and some advice.

"Listen, we're selling the race cars," Cole said. "Go and buy one of them."

When Trybulec inspected the car prior to purchase, he discovered the old blue-and-white paint job where the gold paint had chipped away under the rear bumper. This positively identified the car as the long-lost racer. *Joe Trybulec*

Rohrer bought a 1957 Corvette on May 10, 1958. It was definitely a used race car—with the roll bar still installed—but it was theoretically new because it had never been sold or titled to anyone besides Chevrolet.

"At the minimum, I knew it was a one-owner fuelie car," Trybulec said. "So I told Rohrer's son, Erik, who lives in Colorado, that I'd like to see the car. He couldn't make it to Chicago on such short notice, but he arranged for me to meet his brother-in-law at the father's house.

"When we opened the garage door, I discovered a gold-colored Corvette. But upon closer examination, I could see the white-and-blue-striped paint job underneath where the paint had begun the flake off from age."

Kayser helped Trybulec identify the car. They were looking at the missing Sebring car—the one that had eluded and confused collectors for forty-six years.

"The brother-in-law asked if I wanted to go into the basement to see some of the documentation they also had," Trybulec said. "In that stack of paperwork, I discovered this very car had been used for initial four-speed testing."

"I really want to buy this car," he told the brother-in-law.

"Well, you'd better talk to Erik in Colorado," he said.

While Trybulec was rummaging through the basement of

Rohrer's house, he found a number of items typical of a man the age of the Corvette's owner: an Army uniform from the Korean War, old cameras, and pictures, but then something really caught his attention.

"On the floor, I saw wooden Indian plaque," Trybulec said. "It was exactly the same wood shop project I had done in high school. It turns out that Mr. Rohrer and I went to the same school, the Albert G. Lane Technical High School in Chicago, although I went there twenty years later."

Trybulec waxed nostalgic about his old alma mater.

"We had six thousand boys in our school. It was based on a thirty-four-acre campus and had two metal foundries, two metal shops, two wood shops, and a terrific sports program."

Trybulec hoped he could spin this happy coincidence to his favor.

"I called Erik and told him I'd like to buy the Corvette; that it was a very important car," he said. "But I told him at the very least I'd like to have the Indian plaque. It connected me with his dad, and ironically, his mother was from Arkansas, where I now lived."

Trybulec accomplished what so many barn finders are unable to do: establish a relationship on some other level, about some other topic.

"He told me I could make an offer, but that he already had two other offers," he said.

Trybulec made Erik a significant cash offer, which he knew would be higher than either of the other two offers he had received so far.

"I'll have to talk it over with my sister," Erik said, even though it was clear that Mr. Rohrer had left the car specifically to his son.

"I also need to tell the other two bidders," Erik said.

"I told him I didn't want to get into a bidding war," Trybulec said.

Not surprisingly, Erik called Trybulec back after he told the other two bidders of Trybulec's significant cash offer. They both countered with offers $10,000 higher.

"So I thought for a minute," Trybulec said. "Then I offered him my final deal. I said that I would make him a one-time cash offer, and if he accepted it, the car was mine. I told him I could come to Chicago next week to pick it up."

The following week, as Trybulec was driving up to Chicago to pick up "his" car, Erik called him.

"He said 'I felt the honorable thing to do was to let the other two bidders know of your offer,'" Trybulec said. "My heart stopped beating."

One of the other bidders, who had been intent on owning the Corvette, apparently started becoming very aggressive with Erik.

"What are you, stupid?" said the other bidder. "That's the missing Nassau/Sebring car!"

Erik said, "I don't know you, but I don't like you. The car is Joe's [Trybulec]!"

When he got to Chicago and met Erik, Trybulec found out more about the car and about the relationship between Erik and his father. When Erik was a child, his father had always told him to stay away from the car. Erik hated the car and couldn't wait to get rid of it.

Trybulec couldn't help but believe that the lucky coincidence of the high school had helped him acquire the car. Trybulec loaded up the car and trailered it home.

The promoters at the Bloomington Gold Corvette show wanted him to display his newly found car in as-found condition.

"That made me nervous," he said. "I had been to Bloomington at least twenty-five times, and all the cars were mega-bucks restorations."

But Trybulec's unrestored barn find was one of the most popular cars in the show.

Then he got a call from GM's racing manager, who said they were interested in helping him identify the car and its components. The manager also offered to help me with anything I needed.

"I told him I wanted photos of the car," Trybulec said. "He said they would search through GM's archives and get back to me."

When GM got back to him, he couldn't have been more pleased. His car had set the world speed record for its class at Daytona Beach and had finished first-in-class, fourth overall, at the New Smyrna Beach road race when Paul Goldsmith drove it to finish behind Carroll Shelby, Lance Reventlow, and one of the Holman-Moody Thunderbirds. At first the GM archive search turned up sixteen photographs, but ultimately more than six hundred photos were turned over to Trybulec. They were mostly of his car, but also of other period Corvette race cars. He also received six vintage videos of his Corvette racing.

Suddenly, his phone was ringing off the hook with calls of congratulations and offers to buy.

But it's not for sale.

"I'm inclined to leave the car the way it is and not restore it," he said. "Not that I don't appreciate restored cars, but this one hasn't been driven since 1967 and is one hundred percent authentic."

The only thing he might one day consider is to remove the gold paint.

"The white with blue paint under the gold is perfect," he said. "If I could remove the gold without damaging the original paint, I might try it."

And, quite possibly, his good fortune in owning the car is because of a lucky wooden Indian plaque.

Lucky indeed.

After trailering home his new booty, Trybulec decided he will likely keep the Corvette as-is—100 percent authentic—rather than restore it. He may, however, attempt to remove the gold paint one day. *Joe Trybulec*

CHAPTER SIX

Family Jewels

Help Stamp Out Hot Rods!

Russ Roberts' passion for finding old vehicles dates back to 1955. His lengthy list of barn finds includes motorcycles, trucks, sports cars, muscle cars, and old beaters. Some of his more remarkable finds include a 1951 chartreuse Henry J, a 1949 Willys Panel with a Studebaker V-8, and a 1954 Buick Skylark convertible that he bought for $60 and drove home. He has found fifty-one motorcycles, including three Indians, six BSAs and Triumphs, and eighteen Harleys. Roberts' first car was the 1941 Ford business coupe he bought in 1955 when he was growing up along the Erie Canal in New York State.

"I've spent a lifetime chasing down and saving many autos and motorcycles, and getting them running," said the sixty-six-year-old, who has lived in Eugene, Oregon, since attending the University of Oregon in the mid-1960s.

Russ Roberts poses proudly next to his 1939 Ford convertible around 1956. Because he grew up near the Watkins Glen racetrack in New York, he installed a leather strap across the hood, much like the racing Jaguars of the day. *Russ Roberts*

Of all the cars on Roberts' list, a few qualify as, "Darn, I wish I hadn't sold it!"

"In 1956 I bought a 1939 Ford convertible when I was sixteen years old from a guy who bought it from a couple of sailors who drove it from California to New York with 4.44 rear end gears and Ascot knobby-type dirt track tires," he said. "It had been drag raced, so it was pretty clapped out. It had a worn-out Carson Top that had probably been installed in the late 1940s or the early 1950s."

He paid $75 for the Ford.

He immediately began to work on the car, installing a 303-cubic-inch Oldsmobile engine, which overpowered the stock three-speed Ford gearbox.

"I blew a lot of transmissions, needless to say," said Roberts.

A previous owner had removed the original '39 Ford front end sheet metal and installed a 1940 Ford DeLuxe front end, which Roberts said was a common swap in the 1950s. Once the fenders were in place, he used his mother's Electrolux vacuum cleaner to spray on the dull coat of gray primer paint and hand-painted a couple of eyeballs on the hood.

Among his other automotive accomplishments, Roberts is proud of the photos he took at the sports car races at Watkins Glen road race course.

"I'd go there every year and watch the Allards and Cunninghams race right through town," he said.

The influence those exotic sports cars had on Roberts can be seen in one of the pictures in his scrapbook, which shows the '39 Ford with taped headlights and a leather belt across the hood, similar to an Allard or an XK120 Jaguar.

The racing Roberts did with the Ford, though, was not very exotic. He drag raced it on Friday and Saturday nights on the street. In a fit of adolescent humor, Roberts painted on the left-side sun visor: "Help Stamp Out Hot Rods!"—a sentiment he copied from a protest sign posted in front of a farmer's house near the airport drag strip.

In the middle of his fun with the Ford, the U.S. Navy attracted Roberts to sign up. He parked his convertible in the family barn in December 1957, next to his brother's Olds-powered 1949 Chevy and Chrysler-powered 1949 Ford.

The beloved Ford gathered dust for a year, after which Roberts sold it in 1958 for $350.

"I don't even know why I sold it," he said, "but I did."

After a stint in the Navy, Roberts and his wife lived in San Francisco, then moved to Eugene, Oregon. He enrolled in the

Thirty years after Russ sold the Ford, John Roberts found what he thought might have been his younger brother's old hot rod in the storage shed of an upstate New York car dealer. *Russ Roberts*

The car was positively identified by the "Help Stamp Out Hot Rods" lettering on the driver's side sun visor, which Roberts painted there in about 1956. *Russ Roberts*

University of Oregon in 1961, where he majored in economics, and embarked in a career that started in motorcycle mechanics and later turned to engineering and then surveying.

Years later, when he would gather with friends for a beer and talk about the cars they regret selling, Roberts would always bring up the Ford and show them the worn photo in his wallet.

Decades passed.

One day Roberts' brother John called with some unexpected news. John said that while talking to a used car dealer in upstate New York, he came across a surprising discovery.

"He had a chopped '39 Ford rumble-seat convertible in a leaky shed," Roberts said. "My brother said, 'Oh my God, I think that's my brother's car!'"

The car had rested many years inside the shed. Humidity caused the fabric to peal away from the headliner, shreds of which hung from the old Carson Top–like stalactites. But his brother wasn't sure this was the exact car because so much time had passed since he had last seen it.

Then he flipped down the sun visor and saw a forgotten message: Help Stamp Out Hot Rods!

This was the real thing, the exact car that his brother had sold in 1958. John discovered the car in 1988.

"He said, 'Hey, I found your old '39 convertible,'" said Roberts. "So I told him to see if the guy wanted to sell it. John told me that the guy had stars in his eyes; he thought he had a gold mine."

The car dealer wasn't willing to part with this rusty relic easily. He had recently returned from the huge flea market at Hershey, Pennsylvania, and someone had told him the car was quite valuable. John was able to persuade him to take a 1928 Dodge Brothers sedan in trade along with some cash. Roberts figures the car cost him $2,800 between the old Dodge and the cash. Considering its now-awful condition, he thought he was paying top dollar.

Interestingly, when the car dealer dug out the title, it was still in Roberts' name.

Roberts' brother John, who was in the auto recycling business, had the '39 Ford transported cross-country on his nearly new car hauler by his two teenage sons, Jeff and C.V. Roberts is proud that his nephews delivered the car even though they were only in high school.

"Since it sat in John's barn for a while, the car was totally covered in bat shit," said Roberts. "Really bad. Then it sat in a lean-to at my house until I had the time and money to fix it."

Roberts came up with a plan to pay for the convertible's restoration without dipping into the family budget: He began buying and selling Harley-Davidson motorcycles and pickup trucks.

"I'd always keep the profits and put them toward the next purchase," he said.

Eventually, he had the money required to begin the refurbishment.

"The floors needed to be totally cut out and replaced," he said. "And the firewall was a mess because someone had installed some kind of goofy battery box. I bought a used cowl with a good firewall from a flea market and replaced it. The doors were also rotted at the bottom and had to be repaired."

"I couldn't have done it if I hadn't met Ron Beard. At the time, he was looking for a big fabrication project like mine, and he did a great job."

The car took about two years to restore. Roberts steered clear of using fiberglass replacement parts, preferring instead to either

The car as it looks today. Roberts restored the body to the condition it was in during his high school days, but modified the chassis and drivetrain so it could keep up with modern traffic. *Russ Roberts*

patch or replace the original component. As Beard worked on the bodywork, Roberts and a couple of friends constructed the chassis. They installed a late-model Mustang suspension with rack-and-pinion steering and disc brakes. Roberts installed an overhauled Ford 302-cubic-inch engine and a C4 automatic transmission originally used in a state police car.

The car is finished in a semi-gloss version of Washington Blue, giving it a nostalgic look.

"The car looks so good that it could have looked exactly like that in the 1940s," he said.

Roberts is proud to once again own his high school ride. He uses it regularly and even drag raced it once. He is also happy to have his story recorded here. Now, he says, "I might be known as an automotive archeaologist, and not just a weirdo car nut, which some people know me as."

Finding a Friend's Old Hot Rod

Gary Engberg and his cousin Norman Nelson bought the 1940 Ford standard coupe after seeing it advertised in a local farm newspaper, right next to ads for plows and manure spreaders.

"I was fifteen or sixteen years old, my cousin was a couple of years older, and I think we paid about two hundred fifty dollars for it," said Engberg, a Minnesota native who now lives in Tennessee. "We read too many hot rod magazines, and had to own one. Norman had the money and I provided the encouragement."

The cousins went out to a farm at the outskirts of their little town of Detroit Lakes in northern Minnesota, and literally bought the car out of a barn.

"When we brought the coupe home, we had to clean all the straw and corn cobs out of the trunk," Engberg said.

The year was 1957.

The pair built a hot flathead engine and installed it in the coupe.

"We started with a 1950 Mercury engine, which had the four-inch stroker crank," he said. "We loaded the crankshaft, rods, and pistons into the trunk of our car and drove them to Minneapolis to get the machine work done. We overbored by .120 of an inch and had it balanced."

When they assembled it back home, they installed three two-barrel carburetors and Fenton high-compression heads.

"It was during the days when everyone was putting Chevy engines in their hot rods," he said. "But we could keep up with the Chevys. We lived in a resort area, and in the summer, lots of visitors would come through town with hot cars. Our coupe was always the car to beat."

Norman went into the military in 1960, so Engberg wound up with the coupe. All the street racing started to take its toll on the old flathead engine, and eventually it cracked a cylinder. That summer, out came the flathead and in went a 303-cubic-inch Oldsmobile

Gary Engberg's 1940 Ford standard coupe sat in this Minnesota barn for more than thirty years. Engberg's childhood friend Doug Anderson discovered the coupe just a half-mile from where he grew up.
Doug Anderson

engine. It was hooked up to the stock three-speed Ford transmission, so Engberg kept plenty of extra gearboxes in stock.

"With the car's light weight and all that torque, there wasn't anything that could take it," Engberg said. "One Sunday, a guy with a '51 Ford said his car was hot, so we went out to the four-lane so see who was faster. Well, my hood wasn't fastened correctly, and it flew off at about one hundred miles per hour. We won the race, but that hood took off super high in the air."

Engberg eventually got married and started a teaching career. He drove the coupe into the late 1960s, then parked it in one garage, then another. Eventually, in the 1970s, he sold the coupe after he lost storage.

If you're thinking at this point that Engberg found his old coupe again, you'd be wrong. His cousin Norman didn't find it either.

Doug found it.

Anderson is modifying the car with a 406-cubic-inch engine and air conditioning, and he hopes to drive it from Tennessee to Minnesota for a homecoming. *Doug Anderson*

Doug Anderson used to hang around Engberg's garage when he was a kid. He was a couple of years younger than Engberg and used to help work on the coupe.

"This kid Doug was a nice guy, and we'd let him drive the coupe once in a while," Engberg said.

Evidently those drives left a strong impression on the youth.

"Gary and his brother owned a little speed shop when I was a kid," Anderson said. "I'd walk a half-mile in below-freezing temperatures to hang around there. The last time I remember seeing the car was in 1962. Gary got married and I got married."

"We all lost touch with each other after we went to the military and started families," Engberg said.

Fast forward to December 2005.

"One day I called Gary to see if he knew where his old '40 Ford coupe went," said Anderson, who now runs an engine remanufacturing business in Nashville, Tennessee. "Gary said no, but that I should talk to a guy named Ronnie, who owned the Subaru dealership in

Detroit Lakes and had a nice old Ford collection. Ronnie said, 'Sure, that's right up the street from where you used to live!'"

Anderson was on a quest. It turns out that the car had been sitting in a barn a half-mile from the house where he grew up, and hadn't moved for twenty-six years. The farmer said his son had purchased it with the intention of restoring it, but he also got sidetracked with marriage and career. The farmer had hoped his son would finally sell the old coupe.

"I called the farmer's son, and he said he'd sell it, so I asked him what he thought it was worth," said Anderson. "He said eight thousand dollars, but because the roof had some dents in it when a barn collapsed around it, I offered seven thousand dollars. We split the difference and settled at seventy five hundred."

Anderson sent a check, and when it cleared, the farmer began the long process of removing the car from the barn. It was still all there, and still rust free.

Anderson was delighted. He had owned many fast cars—GTOs, a Hurst Olds—but never a street rod. Now he had the '40 Ford standard coupe he had tinkered on and even driven a few times as a kid. The first hot rod that made an impression on him was now his first hot rod.

Beginning in March 2006, he began the coupe's transformation by installing a new frame, a 406-cubic-inch Chevy engine, a mohair interior, air conditioning, and power rack-and-pinion steering. He's building the car to drive, and he plans to drive it back toward Minnesota for a homecoming.

Is Engberg jealous that he didn't find his old car? Not at all.

"I'm just so happy he's got it," he said. "He's one of our gang. We were so close back then, and to this day. All of us are just as happy with Doug getting the car."

Honoring a Pact

Every soldier returning from Vietnam came home with a story. Some of those stories have been told, but many will sit quietly in the minds of veterans and never be spoken. Glenn Herr carried a story in his wallet for nearly a decade after leaving the service, and has kept it in his heart ever since.

Rather than risk getting drafted, Herr left college on November 1, 1963, and enlisted in the Army Air Corps.

"I knew I was probably going to get drafted, so I joined because I didn't want to be fighting on the ground," Herr said.

Always a car guy, Herr was a mechanical engineering student at Youngstown State College in Ohio when his father rewarded him with a sporty 1960 Ford Starliner. But in a youthful act of indiscretion, he totaled the Ford just before going into basic training at Fort Leonard Wood in Missouri. The accident left Kerr without a car, but he had another possession waiting for him when he returned home: a fifteen-foot Yellow Jacket Fury molded birch ski boat with a Mercury Mark 55A outboard engine. After completing his basic training, he was off to Fort Eustace in Virginia for secondary training, then California, before being shipped out to Vietnam. It was during this time that Herr missed out on one of the most important new car launches in history: the 1964 ½ Mustang.

Because of his mechanical interests, Herr became a helicopter mechanic and worked on Huey choppers. In this position he met another Huey mechanic and fellow car enthusiast, Tom. Before enlisting, Tom had purchased a new car that Herr had never heard about before, the new Ford Mustang.

"I never saw one. I hadn't even heard about the Mustang until he told me he bought one three months before enlisting," Herr said. "We became great friends. Cars were all we talked about. There were other car guys who worked with us, but they were Chevy or Mopar guys, and they'd give us a hard time. We were Ford guys."

Glenn Herr made a pact with a fellow soldier in Vietnam, and as a result he became the owner of this original Mustang convertible years later. He restored the car and won many awards, but ultimately sold it to put the war behind him. *Glenn Herr*

Tom quickly educated Herr about his new car. It was a silver convertible equipped with a 289 engine, automatic transmission, luggage rack, an eight-track tape deck, and fog lights. Even before laying his eyes on an actual Mustang, Herr became a fan of the model.

Over the six months that they worked side-by-side on helicopters, the two mechanics became best friends. In fact, the two made a pact: If either of them didn't make it home from Vietnam, the other could have his most prized possession. In Herr's case, it was his Yellow Jacket ski boat; in Tom's case, it was his new Mustang. They both signed a promissory note and put a copy in their wallets.

Tom also told Herr of the tough life he had escaped in his native Philadelphia. His mother had been an alcoholic and his parents divorced when Tom was a boy. Tom credited his elderly grandmother with raising him on Philadelphia's east side. In fact, his prized convertible sat waiting for him in the shed behind her house.

In 1964, helicopter mechanics made a salary of only $90 per month, but that salary could be increased to a whopping $250 per month if they added as few as five hazardous duty assignments to their normal duties. So the two friends signed up to be "crew chiefs," meaning they would be gunners on the Huey helicopters.

"It was on December fifth," Herr said, "when I signed on as starboard [right] gunner and Tom signed up for portside [left]. We were about thirty-five or forty minutes into the flight and were just north of Vung Tau."

The next few moments have played on Herr's mind countless times.

"We were setting down in a field next to a downed helicopter," he said. "We had hoped to get it running and fly it back to base.

"We were about ten feet above the ground when we came under severe hostile fire from the left side with a fifty-caliber gun. Tom got hit and was almost blown in half. The next round ricocheted off the door handle, and a piece of that handle flew into my flak vest. The force blew me out of the helicopter and I fell about ten feet to the ground. I was unconscious."

The chopper pilot called for emergency firepower and then landed in the field.

"They threw me and what was left of my buddy into the helicopter and we flew back to Saigon," he said. "I was admitted into the hospital, but was released on the same day. They sent me to Bangkok for a week of R & R before I returned to duty."

Things were never the same for Herr. He had lost his best friend, the guy he would spend hours talking to about Fords.

Herr went through the motions for the next four or five months in Vietnam, and he was eventually transferred to Fort Eustace to teach.

"After discharge, I went back to Youngstown State to finish college in September 1966," he said.

Herr immediately treated himself to a new car. In honor of his friend, he purchased a brand new 1966 Mustang loaded with nearly every option. His Forest Green K-Code convertible was equipped with a high-performance 289 engine, four-speed transmission, luggage rack, and deluxe interior.

After graduation in 1971, fresh with a diploma in mechanical engineering, Herr landed a job with Caterpillar in Peoria, Illinois.

"It was in either 1971 or '72 that I went to a trade show in Philadelphia for Caterpillar," Herr said. "I had tried to call Tom's grandmother many times over the years, but she was an old lady who didn't own a telephone. So I stayed a couple of days after the show to see if I could find his grandmother.

"I found the house, knocked on the door, and was greeted by a gracious elderly woman."

For the next two hours, the two talked about the war, and about his relationship with her grandson, Tom.

"I told her I was right next to her grandson when he took his last breath," he said. "And I told her of all the nice things that Tom had told me about his grandmother."

It was then that Herr opened his wallet and removed the yellowed piece of paper that Tom had scribbled on so many years earlier.

"She knew nothing of the deal we had made," Herr said, "but she instantly recognized her grandson's handwriting.

"She broke down and cried."

Tom's grandmother walked Herr out to the dirt-floor shed, opened the door, and revealed the Mustang that had sat idle all these years, waiting for its owner to return.

Grandma didn't know where the paperwork for the car was, but without hesitation gave the car to Herr. He opened the door and saw a decade's worth of "mice poop," but otherwise a rust-free silver Mustang with only 18,000 miles on the clock.

"She was happy that a friend of her grandson was getting the car," he said.

Herr rented a truck and trailer and towed the car back to Ohio, where he lived at the time.

His old friend's silver Mustang wouldn't be alone. Herr had bought seven more Mustangs after purchasing the Forest Green convertible. All eight were housed in the shop behind his house.

"I was thinking ahead," Herr said. "It was my intention to build a collection of Mustangs to help pay for my son's college education."

Herr's son was still an infant.

Herr brought his new convertible into the shop with the intention of getting it running, and then cleaning, painting, and using the car.

"But the engine was junk," he said. "The oil in the crankcase contaminated the bearings, so it needed a rebuild. It turned into a full-blown restoration."

According to Herr, the Mustang was museum quality when the restoration was completed in 1976. He used to visit Ford dealers and purchase outdated Mustang parts and accessories from their inventory at greatly discounted prices. So he installed many of those parts and pieces onto the convertible—which he changed from silver to Ember Glo (red orange)—adding a four-barrel carburetor, deluxe interior, five-spoke rims, and rare factory suitcase covers that mounted on the luggage rack.

He now faced a dilemma: His friend's convertible was finally restored to a very high standard, but Herr had hoped to buy a new house, so he made a tough decision to sell the car.

"It was necessary to sell the car. Keeping it was not an option," he said.

Herr drove the spectacular convertible to the Mustang Club's annual convention in Washington, D.C. His intention was to enter the car in the concours, but show officials prohibited show cars from displaying for-sale signs, so instead he parked it in the car corral area alongside scores of other Mustangs that were for sale. But his Mustang attracted unusual attention.

"After an hour of so, I had a parade of spectators and judges coming to see the car," he said. "Four judges asked me to move the car over to the concours area, but I reminded them that the car was for sale, and that their rules prevented signage in the show."

The car that ultimately won the concours award was a nice but rather plain-Jane black six-cylinder convertible. Apparently, the winning car's restoration had just cost the owner $35,000 to complete.

Herr was asking $32,000 for his fully accessorized convertible.

"The guy with the black Mustang came over to the car corral and looked the car over really carefully," Herr said. "Then he made me an offer of thirty thousand dollars. We settled at thirty-one thousand dollars and the car was his.

"I had put the whole Vietnam experience behind me, and this car was part of it."

But the story isn't over. When Herr attended another industry trade show in Baltimore, he rented a car and drove up to grandma's in Philadelphia to visit and tell her of the convertible's restoration.

"This was the last time I ever saw her," he said. "She died the next year."

But remember the Forest Green convertible he purchased new in honor of his Vietnam friend, Tom? He never sold it, and eventually gave it to his son, Gregory, who owns it to this day.

"I have photos of my wife and me getting married in that convertible, of Gregory coming home from the hospital as a newborn, of Gregory getting married, and *his* son Gabriel Wyatt coming home from the hospital," Herr said.

"I still think about Tom frequently, and about the car he gave me," he said, as he begins to get emotional.

"Let's not even go there."

Father Knows Best

By Joe D'Introno

While I was in college, I worked in a local liquor store. The store attracted all sorts of characters, and everyone who came in had a story to tell. One such gentleman, Cyril, was involved in his family's import business, mostly bringing over goods from Italy. One month it would be cheese, the next tomato sauce, and the one after that, coats.

It was a cold January evening and my girlfriend and I were driving my car on Northern Boulevard in Flushing, Queens, when a purple sports car zoomed by me on the left. Now, it was 1976, and seeing any kind of exotic car in Queens was indeed a rarity. Out of the corner of my eye, I saw two things: a prancing horse and a license plate. It wasn't a New York plate; it was black and had the prefix RO in white. I knew immediately it stood for ROMA. I was nineteen years old, and I had my first feeling of what it might feel like to have a heart attack.

I stepped on the accelerator and was able to catch the phantom Roman at the next traffic light. I pulled up next to the car and peeked over. Oh my God, it was Cyril, my importer customer who frequented the liquor store where I worked.

Our conversation went something like this:

"Cyril, what happened to the tomato sauce?"

"Not this month; we're doing cars."

"Cyril, do me a favor: Drive the car to my house; I want to show my father."

"OK, no problem. Wanna race?"

My girlfriend, now my wife, was with me. She asked what kind of car Cyril was driving.

"That, my dear, is an Italian work of art at its best." My heart was pounding at the sight. "That is a Ferrari 365 GTB/4, front engine, twelve cylinders, six two-barrel carburetors."

She just rolled her eyes as we headed to my house.

The Ferrari pulled into my driveway and it looked beautiful. Cyril and I chatted briefly in the driveway, and he said, "Joe, jump in the passenger seat, and we'll go for a ride."

"Where are we going to go?" I asked.

"Just around the block, but before we go, I am going to place a one hundred dollar bill on the dashboard, and you try to take it off," he said.

So I reached over and took the $100 bill.

"No, no, funny guy," he said. "Wait until I take this baby through the gears, and then try to grab it."

Cyril started the car, and I was in heaven. I was thinking about all the car magazine road tests I had read about cars like this, and I was wondering if I just wet myself.

We turned around the corner and came to a stop.

"Ready?" Cyril asked with a devilish grin.

"*Andiamo*," I replied.

Well, the word wasn't out of my mouth before my back was plastered against the seat as the car took off like a rocket. The whole ride was probably an eighth of a mile on a side street in Queens, but to me it was an emotional event. Around us, cars, trees, and houses blasted by. The ride was over in a blink of an eye, and still the hundred was on the dashboard.

As we headed back to the house, I asked Cyril what his plans were for the car.

"I'm going to sell it," he said.

"How much are you asking for it?" I asked as my palms began to sweat.

"Well, realize that there are spare parts that are included: six extra carburetors and all new brakes. So I'd have to get seven thousand dollars."

I was thinking to myself that a new Corvette costs $10,000, and a used Ferrari with only 9,000 kilometers on the odometer was a flat-out steal.

When we pulled up to my driveway, my father was waiting.

He had been drinking that night and I now realize that Cyril and I should have just kept driving, but we didn't.

"Dad, take a look at the car Cyril just brought over from Italy," I said.

My father came over from Italy in 1952, and he was always quick to point out how anything the Italians did was great and everything from Italy was the best. I thought to myself that I should present the facts of the situation and maybe, just maybe my father would have a soft spot in his heart for this Ferrari.

I was wrong.

"Hey Dad, take a look at this car. It looks great, doesn't it?"

"What exactly do you do with a car like this?" Dad said. "It's good for nothing. It's too much up front, not enough trunk. How do you drive it in the snow?"

Oh, no, I thought, this is not going well. I better jump in.

"Dad, you know Cyril is selling the car."

"So what do you want with me?" he responded sarcastically.

"Dad, you know, you could buy this, and I'll pay you back every cent plus interest, no matter how long it takes. We don't have to drive the car; we could just park it in the garage and keep it as a piece of artwork.

"He only wants seven thousand dollars for the car."

My father looked like he was going to pop a blood vessel.

"Do you know that you could buy a nice, new Buick with that kind of money?" he said.

"But Dad, these cars appreciate in value."

My father was moving in for the kill, and the Ferrari was going to slip through my hands.

"You know, for a kid in college, you're not too smart," he said. "I get seventeen percent interest in the bank and have a brand new Buick in the garage.

"I don't need this piece of junk."

It was over. Cyril drove out of the driveway and the car was soon sold.

The following month I drove past Cyril's house, and in his driveway was a red Pantera with "Gruppo Four" logos on it. I had never seen these markings before, but I had been told these were special Panteras used for racing. Just for fun, I stopped at Cyril's and asked if the Pantera was for sale. He told me yes, $6,000.

I just sighed and walked away. I knew it wasn't going to happen.

Fast forward eleven years. It's the late 1980s, I'm married and have a baby daughter. My parents have retired to Italy. I had amassed enough money that I could actually consider buying a Ferrari during an upcoming vacation to visit my parents.

In Italy, I was told of a Dino, and that got me excited. But when it turned out to be a Fiat Dino, even though it was rare, I became disenchanted. I wanted a real Ferrari.

My father and I took a trip to Lake Como on the rumor that lots of exotic cars were in that region. But when we got there, all we saw were BMWs, Mercedes, and Volvos. I asked a car dealer where all the Ferraris were.

He told me that since the old man died, all the Ferraris were quickly sold.

My father didn't have a clue.

"Old man, what's he talking about?" he asked.

"Dad, he's talking about Enzo Ferrari," I said. "He died about six months ago, and all the Ferraris built during his lifetime have become very desirable and were quickly bought up."

We rode the train south, back toward my father's house. While we were waiting at the station, I purchased a car magazine to pass the time. I was looking at the cars for sale, especially Ferraris. That's when the 365 GTB/4 jumped off the page at me.

"Hey, Dad," I said, "remember about eleven years ago when I brought that Ferrari to the house and you said you'd rather keep the seven thousand dollars in the bank at seventeen percent interest? Well, how much interest do you think you made, maybe seven thousand or eight thousand dollars?"

"Yeah, probably. Why?"

I was going to let my father have it. This was going to be good.

"Well, here is the same car for sale. They're asking seven hundred and fifty thousand dollars."

"Well, you're the guy who went to college," he said. "You know these things; I don't.

"You're the smart guy."

The Winemaker's Bora

Car hunters have been known to travel to remote areas of the country to discover the car of their dreams. Sometimes they go as far away as Russia or Czechoslovakia to take ownership of a long-forgotten car. But every once in a while, some lucky car enthusiast only needs to walk into the backyard.

David Brown is one of those lucky fellows. Brown, along with his sisters, operates Brown Estate Vineyards near St. Helena in Napa Valley, California, which churns out award-winning Zinfandel and Cabernet Sauvignon. Brown is a car guy and one of his favorite stories is about a high-mileage Mercedes diesel sedan—inherited from his father—that he drove while he was in college in northern Michigan.

"It was so cold that winter that my car's battery would always die trying to start the engine when the engine oil was as thick as peanut butter," Brown said. "I was so tired of buying new batteries and having the starter motor rebuilt that I just left the car running all winter."

Obviously, these were in the days when fuel was much cheaper than it is today. The car would just sit idling in the school parking lot outside his dormitory during the day while he was in class and in the evening when he was sleeping. For the entire winter.

Brown doesn't take credit for the global warming crisis, though.

Anyway, Brown has always enjoyed cars. Auto enthusiasm runs in the family. His father Bassett bought a Maserati Ghibli Spyder new in 1969 and drove it to work every day.

"My sisters and I couldn't wait for Dad to come home from work because he would give us rides in his car," he said. "We'd get real excited because we could hear his exhaust from way down the road. I'd sit on the floor and my sisters would sit in the passenger seat."

"I'd drive the three kids around the block after work," said Bassett, sixty-eight. "The Ghibli was such a reliable car when compared to the L88 Corvette I had just prior to it. It was my everyday car, and I put more than a hundred thousand miles on it."

Bassett Brown (center) purchased this dark green Maserati Bora new in New Jersey in 1973. Along with a friend in the yellow Bora, he drove it back home in Los Angeles. Here, a state trooper wonders what all the hurry is about.
Bassett Brown

The mid-engine Bora is not traveling so fast these days. It is housed in a shipping container on the Brown family winery near Napa Valley. Bassett's son David plans to have the car roadworthy again soon.
Tom Cotter

Eventually, though, Bassett decided to retire the Ghibli and buy another new Maserati—a Bora—in 1973. Instead of just going to the dealership, though, he ordered it directly from Italy, picked it up from the shipping ports in New Jersey, and drove it across the United States.

"The Bora never let me down either," Bassett said. "It was my everyday car for years. I don't know why Maserati gets such a bad rap."

When he bought the Bora, he parked the Ghibli in a shed behind the family's Los Angeles home and basically forgot about it. Nearly 100,000 trouble-free miles later, the Bora was also retired and relegated to the shed, replaced with a Mercedes 300SD.

Both cars were squeezed into the shed and were becoming forlorn. The Ghibli hadn't been started in ages, and the Bora was sitting with its cylinder heads removed. They had been sitting there for more than a decade.

When son David graduated from college, he began thinking about fixing up an old car.

"I came home from school in 1994, and the Ghibli was just sitting there looking sad," David said. "I put in a new battery and drove the car for the first time. It hadn't been started in twenty years."

David inherited the Maseratis in 1998.

"My mom said to sell them, but my dad always said he was keeping them for me."

What he inherited was a lot of work. Because the two cars had sat so long, he had to repair nearly every system, including engine, electrical, brakes, interior, and body. Instead of farming out the work to a shop, David rolled up his sleeves and did it himself. The most difficult part was timing the valves on the Bora.

"I had to adjust each cam individually," he said. "But when I finished, I fired it up; it ran fine."

He also replaced the carburetors with fuel injection and tuned it with his laptop computer.

Restoring one Maserati would be quite a chore for any automotive enthusiast, but David is restoring both at the same time.

"It's interesting to me that Maserati went from greatness to relative obscurity, and now the company seems to be making a comeback," he said.

And the torch, along with the torque wrench, is being passed from one generation to the next.

Brown's first Maserati was a 1969 Ghibli Spyder, which he bought to replace his unreliable Corvette. The front-engine Ghibli sits in front of the Bora in the same shipping container. Son David Brown has been restoring the two cars over the past few years. *Tom Cotter*

My Iso Grifo

By Darren Frank

I've always loved cars, and so have my brothers and cousins. We can all cite my dad as the source for this infectious automotive enthusiasm, as he owned and enjoyed a number of sports cars. When I was growing up, he had a late 1950s Corvette. He then graduated to a 1967 Iso Grifo, the subject of this story. The last car he owned, before his untimely death from lung cancer in 1970, was a 1969 Maserati Ghibli.

In 1966, my dad took our family to the New York International Automobile Show at the Coliseum, as he did every year. It was always a treat, but this year was particularly special, because he was now shopping for a sports car. One car that caught his eye was a silver Iso Grifo on the Konner-Brown stand. This is the same model that would later be written up in *Sports Car Graphic*. I still have the picture of it in my photo album.

Later he ordered a new Iso Grifo. We got a call one day to go to the pier in New Jersey to pick up the new car. It was beautiful! The car was green with an off-white interior, had Campagnolo wheels, a Blaupunkt radio, a 350-horsepower motor, a four-speed transmission, and no air conditioning.

This car made a deep impression on me. I used to help my dad clean it on the weekends, a chore I relished. And it was fun to go for drives. I was the only kid I knew whose father owned an Iso Grifo, and I was tremendously proud.

One day, however, my euphoria abruptly ended. A reckless hit-and-run driver caused an accident that resulted in the Grifo being wrapped around a tree. The left front fender was crushed, as was the corner of the car. The front subframe was also damaged. Our dream car was shattered.

Rather than attempt to repair it, my father elected to sell the car. A gentleman from Long Island bought and repaired it in his

Elliott Frank proudly stands beside his new 1967 Iso Grifo in front of his house on Long Island, New York. After an accident, Frank sold the car and the family lost track of it. *Darren Frank*

garage in Hicksville, Long Island. There were rumors that he had converted it to a targa. I heard that his wife worked for Pan Am, and he was able to fly to Italy as often as he wanted to in order to buy the parts he needed.

Despite the many years that went by, I never forgot that green Iso Grifo. It was always a dream to have my own, and I read as many articles on the car as I could. I got in touch with Italian car historian Winston Goodfellow and joined the Iso & Bizzarrini Owners Club. When my father died in 1970, all my hopes of finding his car died with him. I had no idea what its serial number was, who had purchased the car, or how to go about finding it. In 1989 I bought my own Grifo, which I still own and have since completely restored.

One day a few summers ago, I was cruising in my Grifo near my home in Westchester, New York. Someone honked at me, and then started following me in his pickup truck. I thought for sure I had done something wrong or that I had a problem he was going to tell me about. Instead, the driver of the truck explained to me that he had

After giving up hope of ever finding his father's Iso, Darren met Joe Thurstein in 1995. Thurstein had purchased the Iso from Elliott Frank, repaired the damage, and painted it navy blue. *Darren Frank*

a car just like mine at home, only it was dark blue. I told him that he had to be mistaken, that this was a very rare car. No, he said, he was sure he had an Iso Grifo at home, and had owned it for twenty-seven years. He introduced himself as Joe Thurstein. We swapped phone numbers and promised to get together in the near future.

I tried calling Joe several times, but never actually got him on the phone. I left several messages, but he never called back. My wife Kathryn told me to leave him alone—he obviously didn't want to talk. So I did, for a while.

After returning from the 1995 Monterey weekend, I tried calling Joe one last time. We finally connected. He was very glad to hear from me, as he had lost my phone number. He immediately asked me if I was Elliott Frank's son. This had quite an effect on me as my father had been dead for twenty-five years. When I asked how he knew my father, he responded that when I left my full name on his answering machine (and mentioned my interest in the Iso Grifo), he was sure that fate was responsible for bringing us together. Joe was the gentleman who had purchased my father's Iso Grifo back in 1968—and he still owned it!

Oddly enough, this wasn't the first time that Joe had encountered a member of my family in the years following his purchase of the car. He once used a law firm that my older brother worked at (back in the late 1970s). He had talked briefly with my brother about the car once they realized that they knew each other (hence the source of the family "myths" surrounding the car).

Joe assured me that the car was still in his possession. He hadn't driven it in about eight years. It was now blue and all original (Joe felt that green was bad luck, especially for this particular car). Although the Iso factory tried to convince him to convert it to a targa, he hadn't actually done so. Joe and his wife had moved to Northern Westchester, and lived about fifteen minutes drive from where I was living at the time. He said I could come over and visit it whenever I wanted. I did just that the following weekend. The car and I were united again, after twenty-seven years by an incredible coincidence.

My enthusiasm for the car gave Joe the motivation to get the Grifo running and back on the road again. He and I have remained friends over the years, and touch base every so often, despite the fact that my family and I now live in North Carolina. People always ask me if I plan to buy back my dad's Grifo one day, and Joe tells me that when his family is ready to pass it on to the next owner, I'll have first right of refusal. That said, I'm creating my own memories and plenty more for my daughter, Charlotte, with "the red car" (my Grifo, as Charlotte refers to it). That's a family legacy I'll someday pass on to Charlotte, when she's ready for it.

CHAPTER SEVEN

Playboys, Princesses, and Spies

An AMX Fit for a Playmate

By the late 1960s, American Motors Corporation's business was slowing down. The American car-buying public was no longer responding to the style of staid Rambler sedans and wagons. To spur sales, AMC developed economy cars like the Gremlin and the Pacer, but they were mostly seen as odd interpretations to Ford's Pinto and Chevy's Vega.

Seeing that the enthusiast market was devouring performance cars like the Mustang and the Camaro, AMC developed hot versions of some of its lineup, like the Rebel Machine. But the car that was the most radical departure for AMC was the AMX. The AMX was a performance car of the first order; the two-seater came equipped with a choice of several V-8 engines, including a high output 390.

To promote its new performance machine to the male car-buying audience, AMC produced a special Playboy edition painted Playmate Pink and gave it to the 1968 Playmate of the Year, Victoria Vetri, also know as Angela Dorian. Presenting a special car to the Playmate of the Year was an annual tradition, and each year a different car company did so. Over time, Playmates of the Year were awarded a Mustang, a Sunbeam Tiger, a Plymouth Barracuda, a Shelby GT500, and a De Tomaso Pantera.

Vetri's car was equipped with the base 290-cubic-inch V-8 engine, automatic, air conditioning, tilt wheel, AM/eight-track radio, and rear bumper guards. Additionally, a special serial number plate was mounted to the dashboard containing Vetri's measurements: #AMX 36-24-35!

Vetri apparently thought highly of her gift, because she still owns it today, nearly forty years later (although there is no proof that the dash-mounted "serial numbers" are still accurate). But within months of taking possession of her AMX, she had it painted chocolate brown, then gray, then black. This allowed her to drive the car without fear of being followed as a celebrity.

Most AMC enthusiasts believed for a long time that this was the only pink AMX ever produced by the factory.

Apparently a second pink AMX was built in AMC's Kenosha, Wisconsin, plant in October of that year. It spent most of its life far from Playboy's fancy mansions and Hugh Hefner's famous pajama parties. This second pink car lived a quiet life in rural Missouri.

Unlike Vetri's AMX, the other pink car was ordered with the 390-cubic-inch V-8, automatic transmission, black racing stripes, air conditioning, and a leather interior. This car was supposedly used when Ms. Vetri visited the St. Louis Playboy Club.

In early 1969, the second pink AMX had completed its duties, and it was returned to the dealership and sold. Despite its heavy

Records show that only two pink AMXs were built in 1968, one for the 1968 Playboy Playmate of the Year and this one owned by Scott Campbell of Medina, Ohio. *Scott Campbell*

option package, it languished on the dealer's lot until September. The car was purchased by a woman who drove it until she died in 1979. Her stepson then used the car before severely damaging the engine. The stepson was becoming annoyed with folks asking about the AMX sitting in his driveway, so he eventually parked the car under a tree in his backyard until it was sold in 1983. Covered with tree sap, the pink paint had turned black. The new owner used straight gasoline to clean the tree sap from the car in order to prep it for a fresh coat of pink paint.

That owner, though, turned his attention to the restoration of a 1958 Corvette, so the AMX languished in his garage for two decades.

In 2003, Brad Van Zee of Farmington, Missouri, was searching for an AMX to buy and heard rumors of the pink model said to reside in a garage nearby. The car wasn't for sale, but Van Zee pursued it with a vengeance. After a month of negotiations, Van Zee had the pink car in his garage. He completed some engine work and

The AMX is now under restoration. Interestingly, the playmate who received the other pink AMX in 1968 still owns the car today. *Scott Campbell*

general detailing in short order, and the AMX was displayed at the Fiftieth Anniversary of American Motors show in Kenosha in 2004. The car created quite a stir—even though some enthusiasts refused to believe that a second pink car had been produced.

Van Zee wanted to modify an AMX for drag racing, and wisely realized that he would be best off if he found a model that didn't have so much history attached to it. He placed the car for sale and it was purchased by the current owner, Scott Campbell of Medina, Ohio.

Once in his possession, Campbell disassembled the car to evaluate its condition. He determined that the car had been damaged in three separate accidents over the years, and the left front fender and trunk deck had been replaced. The rest of the car, including the trunk and door jambs, had also been hastily repaired and repainted with a very thick coat of paint. Under the hood, under the carpets, and behind the door panels were the only areas where the correct shade of paint existed. The entire exterior of the car will undergo a thorough restoration, but the areas where the original paint existed will be left undisturbed.

The original data plate on the driver's doors is also being preserved with the "00" markings, which designates "special order color."

Campbell hopes to soon have his "other" pink AMX restored to its former glory—good enough for a Playboy Bunny.

The Princess Jaguar SS1

BY MIKE COVELLO, AUTOMOTIVE JOURNALIST

At the 2002 Greenwich Concours, Brian Beni was enjoying the debut of his exceedingly rare SS1 when he noticed a photographer taking an unhealthy interest in his car. The guy spent nearly an hour photographing it. Finally the man approached Beni and said, "I know where there is another one of these cars, here in Connecticut."

"No you don't," retorted Beni, sure that his was the oldest of the three surviving examples from Sir William Lyons' pre-Jaguar car company and the only one in the area.

The man was insistent that an identical car was hidden away just forty-five miles up the Merritt Parkway in Meriden, Connecticut. Given Beni's sixteen-year search for his example, he seriously doubted the man's story, but he was intrigued.

Beni's collection of over forty Jaguars rivals any in the world, and his encyclopedic knowledge of the marque's history makes him a candidate to write a great book. Imagine his surprise when he made the trip to Meriden and learned that the other SS1 was authentic. The Standard Motor Company's chassis No. 135248 supported a Helmut Wing 1932 Swallow SS1 body.

This example of Sir William Lyon's first proper motorcar was sold at the well-known Henleys dealership in London in April 1932 to Prince and Princess Pignatelli of Italy. They delighted in the car's rakish appearance and toured the high society fast lane of Europe throughout the 1930s and 1940s. The happy couple built a beautiful summer home on the shore of Madison, Connecticut, and became respected members of that quaint community.

The Pignatelli's lives, unfortunately, did not remain on this blissful track. The princess was divorced in favor of a younger woman and then lost her sight. The SS1 was put up on blocks in the Madison garage, and there it sat forlornly for twenty years, while the princess remained a much-loved member of the community.

The November 1972 issue of *Hemmings Motor News* piqued W. Haynes Fitzgerald's fledgling interest in antique auto restoration. The advertisement read, "SS Standard Swallow 1933. Offered by Princess Constance Pignatelli, car stored for 20 years, Oakledge, Madison, Connecticut." Fitzgerald's love for detail prodded him to take copious notes of his journey of discovery.

"This was nothing more than curiosity. I never intended to buy the thing," he said.

On the spur of the moment, Fitzgerald decided to take a ride down to the shore, just to satisfy his curiosity. Despite the impressive Island Avenue address and the twin sets of stone pillars flanking the U-shaped drive, the ramshackle house had clearly seen better days. The timid knock on the door was answered by a regal-looking woman who said her mother's car was stored in the carriage house just behind the house.

Fitzgerald fought his way through the underbrush. This was the moment for which car collectors live. What would the sagging garage doors reveal—a rusted hulk, a pristine collectible lovingly tucked away from the ravages of time, or something in between? The SS1 made a good enough first impression that Fitzgerald placed the highest bid, and soon returned, prepared to unearth his treasure.

The Princess had insisted on a photographer being on hand to record the car's removal. The tires were inflated, the blocks removed from under the car, and SS1 was pushed out into the gray November afternoon sun for the first time in at least twenty years.

The huge round headlights almost blinked as the accumulation of dust was swept away. The lines of the car spoke of cross-continental tours and life among European royalty between the two great wars. After the papers were signed and money changed hands, the Princess issued a decree.

"The car must remain black," she said.

As he followed the tow truck back to Meriden, the words echoed in Fitzgerald's ears.

Brian Beni discounted the story about another SS1 in nearby Meriden, Connecticut. But when he finally followed up the rumor and cracked open a sagging barn door, it revealed an honest-to-goodness SS1 once owned by a real princess. *Mike Covello*

Fitzgerald kept an unusually detailed log of his dismantling of the SS1. Besides the copious notes, each assembly was illustrated with an elaborate diagram hopefully showing the path to reassembly. Many of us have made such sketches, but Fitzgerald's are extraordinary. On some of the illustrations, he took the time to ink each knurl of every knob.

Like many projects, the initial burst of energy soon deteriorated into lethargy. The car got pushed aside for other projects until Beni's appearance brought it back to mind.

Like Fitzgerald, Beni also only went to look at the car out of curiosity. He already owned what could arguably be called the finest example of Sir William Lyon's brilliance. What use had he for another? Still, his shock of finding such a rare item so close to his domicile led Beni to purchase the car and transport it back to his home in Pound Ridge, New York. There, Englishman David Davenport and his associate reassembled the pieces for the photos accompanying this story. Soon the car will be returned to its ancestral homeland for a complete restoration, after which Beni's plans are fluid.

There is no doubt that the Jaguar XK120 and E-Type played a larger role in making the world aware of Sir William Lyon's unique combination of "Grace, Space, and Pace." But it's also fair to say that without the SS1 as a starting point there would be no Jaguar motorcars. So it's fortunate that after spending fifty years hidden away, this example will soon be restored to its original splendor.

One further note: When Brian first viewed his new acquisition in the comfort of his own barn, he started to think how sharp the car would look in the dark blue shade that was common in the thirties. Like a thunderclap, the princess's words immediately rang in his head:

"THE CAR MUST BE KEPT BLACK."

Beni's not given to superstition, but why cross a princess? The car will remain its proper shade.

The MG in the Coffin

Jim Snider's outstanding Austin-Healey 3000 started a dialogue that twenty years later yielded him an entombed MG.

"I owned a bolt and screw business," said Snider, of Louisville, Kentucky. "One day a customer of mine came into my office to compliment me on my 3000 that I had parked in my warehouse."

"As I showed him the car up close, he told me of an elderly gentleman out in the country who also owned an old Healey."

Snider always enjoyed meeting fellow Healey owners, so he eventually contacted the gentleman, a gesture that led to a lasting friendship.

The gentleman, Hugh Grundy, and his wife, Frankie, were a fascinating couple. Initially, Snider was intrigued in learning about the Healey 100. The Grundys bought the car new and had modified it with an altimeter and other equipment with the intention of competing in the Mille Miglia sometime in the 1950s. But Snider was equally intrigued to hear about the career that led the Grundys to live for decades in places like Taiwan and Hong Kong.

Hugh Grundy had worked for Air America, a covert airlines operated by the CIA.

Air America hauled supplies, but mainly fought the Communist threat in the 1940s and 1950s. (Interestingly, Grundy's wife Frankie never knew he worked for the CIA.)

Before the Healey 100, there was an MGTC. This was a yellow 1947 model that the young couple used while living in Hong Kong. They traded the yellow MG for a new 1949 black MG. They drove their new sports car around China for a couple of years before having it shipped to the family farm in Kentucky. The farm had been in the Grundy family since the 1700s.

"It was shipped to the farm because Hugh and Frankie thought they were going to stay in Kentucky," Snider said. "Frankie drove it about five hundred miles around Kentucky before the couple moved back overseas in 1964."

The 1949 MGTC in the coffin-like storage container that was built to keep it secure. It was entombed from 1964 until the container was opened in about 2004. With Vaseline rubbed on the chrome pieces, the car was in surprisingly sound condition. *Jim Snider*

But before Frankie left, her dad helped her construct a box—a car-sized coffin—just big enough for the MG. She rubbed Vaseline over all the chrome to protect it for what would be a lengthy storage. But nobody knew just how lengthy it would be.

After Grundy retired to Kentucky, he and Frankie continued their sports car activities, but now in the United States.

The Austin-Healeys brought the Sniders and the Grundys together as friends who would occasionally participate in sports car tours.

"My wife Sharon and I went to dinner three or four times a year with the Grundys, and we became great friends," Snider said. "I had known Hugh for about ten years before I asked him one day while we were out in his barn, 'Hey Hugh, what's in the box?' He told me it was Frankie's old MG, and that someday he'd show it to me."

Original owner Frankie Grundy (left) and new owner Sharon Snider pose for a picture with the MG before transferring ownership. Sharon's husband Jim decided it should be her car because she was born the year the car was built, 1949. *Jim Snider*

Hugh and Frankie Grundy, the original owners of the MG, say goodbye to their longtime (four-wheeled) friend as Jim and Sharon Snider prepare to trailer the car to its new home. *Jim Snider*

"It was another five or six years before he actually opened the box and let me look inside."

What Snider saw in that box was a time capsule: an original MGTC right down to its paint. The car was in needy condition: The paint was old, the tires were flat, and the interior had seen better days. Despite this, the car had been well-preserved for more than four decades, and the Vaseline-covered chrome was still like new.

"I expressed my interest in the MG, but it was Hugh's intention to restore the car," Snider said. "Then, one day, Hugh called me and said, 'You know, I'm ninety years old. I don't think I'll have time to restore it. Frankie and I would like you and Sharon to own the car.'"

Snider was excited, and after promising not to sell the car while the Grundys were alive, he took ownership of the 1949 TC in 2004. Snider decided that the car was going to be his wife Sharon's, since she was born the year the car was manufactured.

Sharon's MG is completely restored now, and it takes a place proudly next to Jim's Austin-Healey. As a tribute to the Grundys—Hugh is now ninety-three and Frankie is eighty-seven—the Sniders kept the original Hong Kong license plate on the car.

The Robber Baron's Bugatti Boondoggle

BY DON SHERMAN, TECHNICAL EDITOR, *AUTOMOBILE* MAGAZINE

The 1964 Shakespeare-Schlumpf transaction is the grandest used-car deal in recorded history.

After Volkswagen AG took over control of Bugatti in 1998, executives at the peoples' car company thought it might be nice to own one of the six Type 41 Royales that Ettore Bugatti created as "the car for kings." Purchasing a Royale Coupe de Ville cost VW an estimated $17 million, a shrewd investment given the estimated worth of Royales today. But contrast VW's deal to one Fritz Schlumpf—in his day, the most ruthless carmonger on Earth—pulled off in 1964: $85,000 for one Park Ward Royale limousine and twenty-nine other Bugattis extracted from a dusty barn near St. Louis, freight to France included.

Fritz Schlumpf, who died in 1989, was a shady character. Born poor, he and his older brother Hans earned a fortune in the textile business. In the 1950s, the two owned four woolen mills, a villa, and most of the homes in the village of Malmerspach, France, in the Alsace region. Their family motto—Acquire, Possess, Dominate—didn't mince words concerning their attitudes toward wealth and workers. During the German occupation in World War II, the Schlumpf factories supplied the wool for Wermacht uniforms.

Upon the passing of his mother in 1957, Fritz was moved to ponder her legacy as well as his own. He concluded that a monument to automobiles in general and to the cars that Ettore Bugatti constructed nearby would be an appropriate tribute to his mother and to the family's region (his mother's passion for cars is unknown; the son's is legendary). A fifth mill was purchased in Mulhouse to serve as the repository for Schlumpf's car collection. Mechanics, carpenters, and upholsterers were hired to refurbish the

John Shakespeare of Shakespeare fishing reel fame began acquiring Bugattis, thirty in all, in the 1950s and parked them in this dirt-floor storage building in Illinois. By 1964, he sold all of them to eccentric Bugatti collector Fritz Schlumpf for $85,000. *David Gulick*

vehicles. By 1965, a staff of forty workers were on hand toiling over seventy Bugattis and 130 other cars Fritz had acquired.

Many of the Bugattis came Schlumpf's way shortly after noted historian and marque enthusiast Hugh Conway compiled a worldwide registry listing every known Bugatti owner in 1962. That served as a convenient mailing list to Schlumpf, who dispatched a solicitation letter to every Bugatti owner listed.

John Shakespeare of Centralia, Illinois, received Schlumpf's missive and mentioned to a fellow car enthusiast that he might consider selling his collection of thirty Bugattis for $105,000, the money he had invested in the lot. He also told a newspaper reporter, "It's awful easy to get too many hobbies. Right now, I'm more interested in sports that I can actively participate in like waterskiing and sky diving."

With near-Internet speed, Shakespeare's conversation reached Conway, who quickly forwarded the scuttlebutt to Schlumpf. He responded with rabid enthusiasm.

"Your communication surprised me as much as it gave me pleasure. Mr. Shakespeare's collection interests me and we are going to try to make this deal," Schlumpf noted.

The deal, according to Schlumpf, was worth $70,000 for thirty cars in impeccable condition, freight included.

Shakespeare's golden spoon upbringing was on the opposite side of the tracks from Schlumpf's bootstrap roots. His father, William Shakespeare, invented two key fishing gear advancements: the level wind reel and the backlash brake. The company he formed at the end of the nineteenth century introduced both monofilament fishing line and fiberglass rods.

Following studies at Harvard graduate school, John settled in Centralia, Illinois, in 1950 to oversee various car dealership and oil business interests. His car enthusiasm began with a Porsche 356 and quickly escalated to Ferraris. He and Luigi Chinetti co-drove a Ferrari 375MM to a sixth-overall finish in the 1954 La Carrera Panamericana road race. A year later, when Briggs Cunningham closed his shop in Palm Beach, Florida, Shakespeare moved in with vague plans to produce his own low-volume sports car.

In 1956, while shopping for cars, Shakespeare discovered the Bugatti legend and promptly purchased a 1932 Type 55 supercharged sports roadster. Mere months later, a St. Louis newspaper headline proclaimed: "Centralia Man Buys Biggest, Costliest, and Rarest Car in the World." In this instance, "costliest" was about $10,000 for a 1933 Bugatti Royale with limousine coachwork by Park Ward and Company of London. Shakespeare drove his prize home, noting that the mechanical brakes didn't slow the 7,000-pound car very well on his 250-mile journey.

Schlumpf had no interest in dealing directly with the seller. Instead, he told Conway, "I'd like to inspect Shakespeare's collection, but don't have the time. Can you go in my place? If not, we'll have to send someone in whom we have complete confidence. There are a lot of bandits in this field of car salesmen."

Conway delivered Schlumpf's $70,000 contingency offer to

Shakespeare and convinced Robert Shaw, the Bugatti Club member living closest to the collection, to conduct a thorough inspection of the goods. Shaw, the only survivor of this epic transaction, not only remembers many details, but also he preserved the correspondence and kindly shared it with me, shedding light on one of the shadiest used-car deals in history.

After acknowledging that five of his cars were disassembled for restoration, Shakespeare invited Shaw to inspect the collection, and he expressed willingness to let it go for less than his asking price—as long as the cars were destined for a suitable new home.

Shaw's first report to home base was disparaging to say the least.

"The Shakespeare collection is housed in a facility formerly used as a foundry. Most of the cars are in a dirt-floored building. The roof leaks, windows are broken, and birds are nesting inside. The better cars are in a heated, concrete-floored shop. Practically every car is in some state of disassembly; none has run in eighteen months," he noted.

"The Royale, the Type 56 electric inspection vehicle, the Type 55 roadster, and the Type 13 three-place light car are in presentable condition. It appears that Mr. Shakespeare was taken advantage of when he purchased others sight unseen. The Type 50 LeMans is a replica of some sort. Another car is made of Buick parts."

Rounding up the spare parts for thirty Bugattis in various conditions was a daunting task. Here, the spare wheels are collected for transatlantic shipping. *David Gulick*

Shaw's recommendation to Schlumpf: Do not buy the collection.

That suggestion was ignored. Conway wrote Shakespeare:

"Mr. Schlumpf is keen and has the workmen to put these cars back in order. He has offered to stand by his price subject to the Royale being roadworthy."

A month later, Schlumpf raised his bid to $85,000. While prepping the cars for shipment, Shakespeare made this disheartening discovery: the Royale's engine block was cracked. Schlumpf's response was to have a mechanic repair the 238-pound lump with arc welding.

Shakespeare was so disgusted by that suggestion and the deal in general that he washed his hands of the sale and left for Florida on vacation.

Shaw, skeptical the transaction would ever take place, was dispatched to save the day. He found that the southern respite had brightened Shakespeare's mood. Annoyed when he learned that Schlumpf already owned several Bugattis, Shakespeare nonetheless resumed assembling pieces—two of his cars were in Florida—and preparing (probably bogus) invoices according to Schlumpf's instructions.

Unfortunately, Shakespeare's efforts were too deliberate for Schlumpf. After his request for a shipping date was ignored, Schlumpf pressed, "I wrote you nicely and prettily without animosity. But you must not confound or translate my prettiness with weakness." The French industrialist threatened to lodge formal complaints through ten institutions ranging from "the American tribunal and court of justice" to "all Bugatti clubs and automobile reviews [magazines] in the world." He set a deadline of four months for shipment and threatened to claim damages of $500 per day if Shakespeare didn't comply.

Shakespeare responded with two months of silence, followed by the hint that his collection might be broken up "to perpetuate the great Bugatti tradition." Soon thereafter, Schlumpf characterized a letter he received from Shakespeare's attorney as blackmail. From the sidelines, Shaw silently cheered Shakespeare for not caving in.

Late in 1963, the quixotic Shakespeare resumed a friendly dialogue as if no harsh words had ever been traded. His progress report to Schlumpf advised that the Florida cars had been moved to Illinois, but he was having difficulty finding new tires for the Royale. Unfortunately, no space was available for shipping the cars until the following spring.

In February 1964, after fourteen months of dickering, Shakespeare told Schlumpf, "Your cars are ready. I am eager to have this transaction completed and when I get the money, I will ship the cars."

Shortly thereafter, three Southern Railway freight cars were backed onto a siding that ran within yards of Shakespeare's storage building. While a mechanic steered, railway workers heaved Ettore Bugatti's personal inspection runabout to a top berth. The car made its final journey on U.S. soil at the end of a chain towed by a Jeep.

David Gulick, then a staff photographer for the *St. Louis Post-Dispatch*'s Sunday Pictures magazine, was present to document the loading process. He coaxed a smile from Shakespeare as the eccentric collector removed the Royale's Brogue chronometer and prancing elephant radiator mascot for separate packing. All the cars were shipped with no protection from damage beyond steering wheel wrappers. At the end of a long loading day, the thirty Bugattis left Illinois en route to New Orleans. There they were transferred to a Dutch freighter bound for Havre, France.

Upon arrival in Mulhouse, "His Highness" Fritz Schlumpf stood armed with a whip to shoo away the curious. There were plenty of onlookers, including journalists who had been pestering the despot for access to his horde after hearing about the Shakespeare cars and fourteen other significant Bugattis he had purchased from Hispano-Suiza.

Two years before, Schlumpf initially denied Conway's wife Eva admission to his collection. When *Automobile Quarterly* editor L. Scott Bailey repeatedly asked for a visit, Schlumpf told him that he was contemplating a press event of epic proportions; on the

Several of the Bugattis were disassembled. Here, mechanical parts are gathered to be put in crates.
David Gulick

condition that no journalist ever request a return visit, each car would be wheeled into the sunlight for fifteen minutes.

Schlumpf treated his employees with equal disdain. Their grievances about working conditions and the diversion of company resources were ignored. In 1972, the rise of socialism prompted bitter strikes. Locked out of their mills and barricaded from their villa, the Schlumpf brothers seized refuge in the mill that had been lavishly refurbished as a car museum. While business conditions deteriorated with rampant inflation, worker unrest, and rising competition from synthetics, the Schlumpfs poured their wealth and energy into their car collection.

By 1976, the museum was ready for its public opening. Since the mills were writhing in debt, the brothers magnanimously offered to sell all their holdings—except the museum—for one franc. That prompted embezzlement charges and threats of bodily harm. The brothers fled to Switzerland and the workers seized control of both the factories and the museum.

Imagine their amazement when the Schlumpf shrine—three football fields in size—was raided in 1977. There were 122 Bugattis and 305 other pristine automobiles parked on carefully laid beds of white gravel. Another 150 cars in storage awaited restoration. Ornate Venice Grand Canal candelabras sparkled from eight hundred roof pillars. Three restaurants stood ready to host twelve hundred diners. The washrooms were lavishly decorated with gilt-edged mirrors.

Tried in absentia for tax evasion, falsified accounting, abuse of assets, and gross mismanagement, Fritz Schlumpf was sentenced to a four-year prison term and fined $10,000. His brother received the same fine with a two-year term. Neither served a minute behind bars.

The museum was liquidated by the courts to pay the Schlumpf's debts. The new owners christened the facility Muse National De L'Automobile in 1982. After the Louvre and the Eiffel Tower, it's one of France's most popular tourist attractions. Most of the collection is still on display today, including some of the Shakespeare cars. But

Workers prepare the cars for transport. Here a plastic cover is fitted over the steering wheel of a Bugatti, which is really all the weather protection each car received. *David Gulick*

you won't find the Royale's elephant mascot or its chronometer. Suspicions are that the Schlumpfs carried that booty to exile.

This story does not end happily for the protagonists. In 1975, Shakespeare was found dead in the basement of his home. The sixty-nine-year-old bachelor had been handcuffed, gagged, and shot once in the head. Police interrogated suspects in ten states and at least three foreign countries but no charges were filed and no arrests were made.

Hans Schlumpf died in 1989. Fritz was allowed only a brief visit to his collection before his death in 1992.

Those who visit the Schlumpfs' museum should keep an eye peeled for one very special car on display. The Type 38 two-place roadster, lovingly "rebodied by Shaw of America," was donated to the collection by the Robert Shaw who preserved this Bugattis-in-the-barn story.

A sight you won't see on an Amtrak train anytime soon, a worker secures the Bugattis on open railcars for transport to New Orleans, where they were placed on a Dutch freighter for La Havre, France. One wonders what this stash would be valued at today. *David Gulick*

Ginger's Hemi in the Barn

Matt McGhee is an enthusiast barn finder. After reading *The Cobra in the Barn,* the seventeen-year-old from Eugene, Oregon, began e-mailing me with regular updates on the cars he had discovered. (This reminds me of my own youthful enthusiasm, when I would keep notepads full of old cars that I had found, along with locations and prices.)

McGhee, who currently drives a 1970 VW Rabbit, works part time at the local St. Vincent de Paul used car lot, where he has detailed a 1966 Mercury Montclair and a 1970 Fiat 124 sedan for resale. He has also located a couple of early 1950s Kaisers, but none seemed worthy enough for inclusion in this book until he mentioned Ginger's Imperial.

That's Ginger as in Ginger Rogers, actress and dance partner to Fred Astaire.

His first note to me started out: "My name is Matthew McGhee, and I'm e-mailing to tell you about this white-over-pink 1955 Imperial Newport hardtop coupe that I came upon when I was in third grade (circa 1998). I received a Hot Wheels model of a 1955 Chrysler 300 for Easter. Then the next day my school bus took a detour and I noticed the pink Chrysler. I couldn't believe my eyes. I recently found out that is was owned by Ginger Rogers (well-known 1950s actress), who owned a dairy farm in the Rogue Valley."

This car, and especially its ownership, got my attention.

Matt went on say that the car is sitting in a dilapidated garage at an abandoned house.

"The car has been sitting since at least 1979. It is not for sale, to the best of my knowledge."

How could I find out more? This was becoming interesting, and I began communicating with Matt on a regular basis.

It seems that Rogers had owned a farm in Medford, Oregon, which must have been a blessed getaway from all the hustle-and-bustle of Hollywood. It is believed that Rogers bought the Chrysler in Beverly Hills in 1955, and soon thereafter either drove it or had it transported to Oregon to use when she visited the farm.

She certainly ordered a beautiful car. It was pink and white with white leather interior. The 1955 Imperial was equipped with a two-speed automatic transmission that shifted through a lever on the dashboard. Under the hood was a 331-cubic-inch Hemi engine with four-barrel carburetor that produced about 180 horsepower.

When Matt discovered the Imperial—not knowing of its celebrity ownership—it was just a neat old car. It wasn't until he mentioned it to a friend, Bob White—owner of an automobile parts and memorabilia store—that he learned of its interesting past. White told him that Rogers owned a farm in southern Oregon, but little of the car's history is known from that time until it materialized in the mid-1970s.

"I owned an identical pink and white Chrysler," said Jerry Bureau, owner of East Amazon Antique Auto Supply. "The only difference was that mine had leather and cloth interior instead of all leather.

"In fact, I tried to buy that car from the owner, but he was never even interested in talking to anyone."

When I spoke with Bureau, which White recommended, he said he hadn't even seen that car in at least twenty years.

"I used to see it out on Eighteenth Street parked in the old garage, but I don't drive in that direction much anymore, and I just forgot about it."

He was surprised that the car was still in the same location.

According to Matt, a large tree had grown up in the driveway, leaving the car hidden from the road.

Matt, ever the detective, did some additional investigating. He told me that the property where the car was stored was owned by George Cole, who also owned Cole Furniture. He even e-mailed Cole's phone number to me.

"Yeah, I own the car," said a gruff voice on the other end of the phone. Cole owned the Imperial, as well as a 1955 Desoto.

"I don't remember when I bought it—twenty, maybe thirty years ago."

"There was an ad in the paper a long time ago. I read the ad and decided to buy it. Our whole family hopped on a Greyhound Bus and bought it from a guy who bought it from Ginger Rogers. I paid for it, and the whole family piled in and we drove it home."

"My son is forty-one years old now, and he was eleven when we bought the car, so I guess I bought it thirty years ago."

Cole used the Imperial for three or four years as his daily driver before parking it.

"I'd like to get it restored someday," said Cole, thankful that he parked the pink and white car inside the dilapidated garage, because the fate of his '55 Desoto, which was parked outside, isn't so good. The car is rusted and rotted and pretty much destroyed. According to White and Bureau, the Desoto, which didn't have celebrity ownership, was a much nicer car than the Imperial when they last saw it twenty years ago. Cole said there is a fellow who has a document by Ginger Rogers verifying her ownership of the Chrysler.

"I suppose I should buy that from him," Cole said.

Well, there you have it, a barn-find story with the all-too-often-heard, "It's not for sale." But Matthew McGhee is undaunted. He's still looking for old cars. He's currently on the trail of a 1939 Tabot Lago T-120 coupe.

Keep me informed, Matt. I'm working on a sequel to this book now.

Old-car enthusiast Matt McGhee discovered this Hemi-powered Chrysler Imperial in an Oregon barn. When he began to ask questions about the car, he discovered that it had been owned by the late Hollywood actress Ginger Rogers. *Matt McGhee*

APPENDIX

Top 20 Barn-Finding Tips

I've been barn finding since I was a kid. In fact, I would make notes of cars I discovered on the way home from school on the bus, then ride my bicycle back there on the weekend to inquire about them. So, many of the barn-finding tactics are second nature to me. But friends and acquaintances often ask me for tips on how they can get started, so I started to keep notes a few months ago and have compiled these twenty tips to help car enthusiasts discover cars while they are on a business trip, vacation, or simply going to the convenience store for a quart of milk.

1. You Can Go Home Again

Chances are that you remember car guys who fiddled with old hot rods, sports, or antique cars in the town where you grew up. Even if you moved away two or three decades ago, that doesn't mean that enthusiast doesn't still live there. As you read in the story on my own barn-find cars, I recently bought an Abarth coupe from the estate of a man who I remembered worked on cool cars in his driveway when I was a kid.

And in *The Cobra in the Barn,* I went back to a house where I remembered an old MGTC when I was a kid riding by on my bicycle to discover that it was still there, three decades later!

2. Saturdays and Sundays Are Best

The weekends are the best time to discover cars that might be hidden in people's garages. That's the time when people do yard work and house cleaning chores, and often open up their garages to take out rakes, shovels, ladders, etc. And guess what? Those cars that are usually hidden behind garage doors are often exposed then. I have often thought that x-ray vision would be the most handy talent to have in searching for old cars. However, searching on weekends is the next best thing.

3. By Car, Yes, But By Foot and Pedal, Too

The easiest method to go barn finding is, or course, by car. Or better yet, truck, because owners of old cars might be less intimidated if you come cruising up to their house in a truck as opposed to a new Lexus or Porsche (a nicely worn pickup truck is not intimidating to anyone). However, I have found that bicycling, walking, and running are also excellent ways to search for cars, especially in densely populated neighborhoods. That's because you can travel a lot slower and more carefully inspect the area. I once discovered a Jaguar XK120 when I lived in Bethpage, New York. I remember telling my wife that I was going for a bike ride and wouldn't return until I found a neat old car older than 1960. I peddled past a house where the garage door was open revealing a pile of bicycles, sleds, and other household goods. But near the bottom of that pile, I saw a taillight that looked like it belonged to Jaguar. I knocked on the door and the man almost fell over when I asked if the Jaguar was for sale. "How did you see the car?" he asked. It was only because I was traveling at a very slow speed that I was able to discover the car.

4. Look Behind Yourself

"Look where you're going!" is what I have heard for more than thirty years from my wife when we're driving. You see, I have a bad habit of looking behind me slightly when I drive past houses and buildings. Unless you plan to eventually drive back in the opposite direction, you'd better look over your left and right shoulders to see what cars you are missing as you drive down the road.

5. Dead End and "No-Outlet" Roads Are Best

Nobody wants to drive down a dead-end street because when you get to the end, you'll have to do a three-point turn to reverse direction and come back out again. So guess what? That means 99 percent of people don't bother going down there. This means that old cars might be lurking there, still undiscovered. Take the road less traveled and you'll strike gold every once in awhile.

6. The Back Rows of Auto Repair Shops and Car Dealers

Having worked in auto repair shops, car dealerships, and auto parts stores, I know that often the most desirable cars are hidden on the back rows, away from most prying eyes. That's where the project cars languish when owners can no longer afford to pay the restoration bills, or where an old parts car from a long-forgotten project still sits. Or where the repair shop owner's old project car has been pushed because a newer one, or a boat, has taken its place. Check out these spots, and I promise you that your time won't be wasted.

7. Talk to Home Delivery People/Policemen

In this book, you met Officer Barn Find. In *The Cobra in the Barn,* you read about a propane deliveryman who discovered a 289 Cobra that I wound up owning. These people—and others whose jobs take them onto private property, legally—are often the best resources for information about cars that sit beyond the view of the street. I've asked my UPS man and my landscaper to keep me informed of old cars they might see on their routes. You might try the same thing, with your mailman, meter reader, or house painter.

8. Check out Old Classified Ads

My wife Pat thinks I'm crazy. "Why are you keeping all those old copies of *Hemmings Motor News?*" she often asks. Well, besides being a pack rat, I actually have a method to my madness. I have an idea of one day having the time to go through old issues of *Hemmings* and looking for cars that I have an interest in. Then, I plan to call the advertiser and ask if the car might still be available. Now, the chance of a car still being available after twenty years is not very likely, but I'm willing to bet that there is an occasional needle-in-a-haystack. Can't you just hear the phone conversation: "Hello, my name is Tom Cotter and I'm just calling to see if that Cobra you were selling for $5,000 in the 1970s is sold. It didn't? OK, I'll be right over!"

9. Write Letters to the Owners of Cars Who Won't Sell

As you've read in the story about the Plymouth Superbird, sometimes a nice letter to the owner works wonders. I have heard of this happening a number of times. When an owner, especially an elderly owner, is reluctant to sell, a nicely written letter has "lasting power." After the owner is deceased, or relatives take over the elderly person's affairs, the situation comes up about what to do with Gramp's old cars. If a letter is part of that person's personal effects, you just might be doing that family a huge favor. After all, they won't need to advertise the car or in many cases, even get it appraised. Occasionally, this method is a real winner, but you have to give it time.

10. Go Car Hunting in the Winter

Going car hunting in the summer is nice, but the winter is better. Why? Because the trees lose their leaves. It's amazing that you can pass the same patch of woods everyday all year long and see nothing but trees. But in the winter, that same patch of woods reveals something metallic that catches your attention. It's a bumper or a fender. And even though cars abandoned outdoors are often in poor condition, who knows? Going car hunting in the winter is almost as good as having x-ray vision because the usual wall of greenery is gone until spring.

11. Reverse Psychology: Ask If They'd Like to Buy Parts

Chances are that a person who has an interesting car visible from the road is used to having people walk up and ask if it's for sale. And their standard answer will most often be, "NO!" Next time, try reverse psychology; knock on the door and ask if they would like to buy parts for their car. Just say that you have some parts for a car like their's, and if they need something, you might be able to help them out. More often than not, it will lead to a longer conversation, which might lead to an answer better than no.

12. A "For Sale" Sign Often Means It's Too Late

I've bought hundreds of cars in my lifetime, and only a couple of them had a "for sale" signs posted on them. That's because if a sign is already taped on the windshield, the owners have probably gone through the thought process and investigated the car's value. The best method is to knock on the door and ask if that old car behind the barn is for sale. Maybe, just maybe, you will hit them off-guard, and you can make an offer on the car, making it easy on the owner. Good luck.

13. Out Buildings behind the House Are a Good Sign

When I'm out cruising around, I not only look for old cars, but old buildings. After all, old cars left outdoors are probably in pretty poor condition. If the car is stored indoors, though, it might be in pretty good shape. Look for a building that has not been used for a long time; one that has ground-level garage doors. No guarantee that a classic car is sitting inside—more often than not, it will be an old John Deere tractor—but it's worth a try.

14. "Can I Use Your Barn For Photography?"

This works especially well if you have a nice-looking old car at your disposal. If you suspect that a barn or old building might contain an old car, drive your old car up the driveway, knock on the door, and ask if you can use their old barn or building as a backdrop for photos of your own car. Most property owners will be flattered and say OK. This will give you the opportunity to peek inside the windows and view what you couldn't see from the street.

15. "Excuse Me; Is This the House with the Old Cars?"

Even though I have never done this myself, I have heard that it works pretty well. I was once told that some car enthusiasts went to the door of a mansion on the bluffs near the Breakers in Newport, Rhode Island. They knocked on the door and asked if this was the house with the old cars. "We were told by an old man downtown that one of these houses had some old cars in the garage. We'd just like to see them," they said. That the first house didn't have any old cars, but that the owner told them that the house next door had some old cars. The car hunters eventually worked their way around the neighborhood, seeing an incredible assortment of cars in one afternoon.

16. Check Airplane Hangars at Small Airports

My friend Peter Egan many years ago wrote a column in *Road & Track* about pilots of small airplanes who are often also car enthusiasts. So I decided to check it out for myself, and son-of-a-gun, there are cars under those wings! Drive into a small airport on a nice Saturday or a Sunday, when hobbyists are working on their planes, and most likely, the hangar doors are open. More often than not, parked under the private plane's wings will be a Bug Eye Sprite, or a Mustang convertible, or some other interesting set of wheels. Often those cars have taken a back seat to the plane and may be for sale.

17. Old Car Parts Lying Around a Garage Are a Good Sign

You might not see a car parked inside the barn, but there are other clues that an old car might be parked somewhere on the property. Look for old gas station signs, gas pumps, or body parts that might be hanging on the side of a building or lying around the property. Often these items show that a car enthusiast lives on the premises, and that something interesting might be lurking out of sight. It takes a trained eye, so keep your vision peeled for odds and ends in the backyard; it might lead to a gold mine.

18. Public Parking Garages

Jay Leno turned me on to this trick. If you live near a major city, especially in the older part of that city, take a tour of some of the pubic parking garages. Leno himself discovered a Duesenberg that had been parked in one spot for more than seventy years, never picked up by its owner! And he's heard of another garage in New York City that may contain a Bugatti that has been parked a similar amount of time. Remember, rich people who live in the city have no place to park their cars except in these garages. When they stop driving, move, or die, those cars are often forgotten and just left. Some of these cars might be available for purchase just by paying the storage fees.

19. Ultralight

It always bothers me when I see a prime piece of property—one that I believe could contain an old car—but I can't see beyond the hedge. Shucks, if I could only fly! One day I saw a guy flying low and slow over my house and I got an idea: What if I got an ultralight plane and flew over farms and country houses and could inspect what is sitting in the "lower 40" that is not visible from the street? I haven't done it yet, but I'll bet someone reading this book has an ultralight sitting in the garage.

20. Talk the Talk, Walk the Walk

Always talk about your hobby to everyone who will listen. If you are known as a car guy, people will give you leads on cars that are in Aunt Millie's garage, often hoping that you'll give them advice on how to dispose of it. I know two semi-car guys in my town—Hugh and Bruce—who knew each other for at least two decades, but neither knew the other guy liked old cars until I told them! This was the case even though they live only two miles from each other, and one has a Jaguar XK120 in his garage and the other has an AC Greyhound in his barn. Don't make this mistake; let everyone know you pay homage to the car gods.

INDEX

INDEX